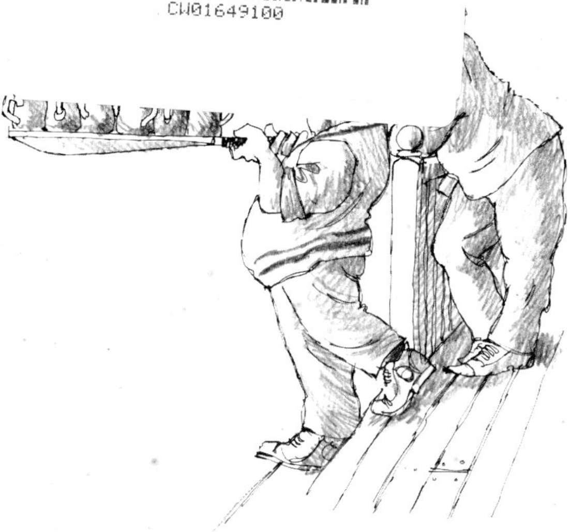

CREAM CAKES AND BOUNDARIES

Village Cricket Tea Recipes

Compiled by
Charmaine Hutton

Illustrated by
Hugh Cushing

To all hardworking Cricket Tea Ladies who faithfully bake, slice and butter every weekend throughout the summer, providing that essential element of the game that we all so look forward to -
the afternoon break for TEA!

First published in Great Britain 1998 by
The Cricketer/Sporting Magazines & Publishers Ltd.
Beech Hanger, Ashurst, Kent, TN3 9ST
Tel: 01892 740256

ISBN 0 902211 08 0

Design By Chris Beasley

Printed in Great Britain by Flexiprint, Lancing, West Sussex

CONTENTS

Cricket is unique, not so much in the manner in which it is played, but more because of the breaks in play. There is no half-time as in Soccer, no quarter-time and three quarter-time as in Australian Rules. Instead, there is lunch and tea at places like Jugiong on the Murrumbidgee River, or Longparish on the River Test. At Jugiong it will consist of strong tea in an enamel mug and sturdy corned beef sandwiches, no tastier though than salmon and cucumber on thin, crust-less brown bread and pale tea from a delicate china cup at Longparish. It is a ritual, you see, and it will be a great pity if the new Millennium fails to embrace it.

Richie Benaud, BBC TV Commentator

Introduction

Being the daughter of a former amateur Somerset cricketer, the wife of an ex-Yorkshire and England professional and mother of two aspiring cricketers a comment I get from many people is: 'I expect you make lots of cricket teas.' Surprisingly I have never had the entire responsibility of making tea for two teams and supporters, but I am sure many have been thrown in at the deep end with no help or guidance.

I hope this book is the answer. I started by asking the experts - 650 tea ladies from the teams in The Cricketer National Village Cricket Championship. The recipes included in this book are just a selection of the hundreds which arrived from all over the country together with their shopping lists. Many are old-fashioned childhood favourites, very quick and easy to prepare. The recipes have been tested by Mary on *The Cricketer* staff, who are all now bowling off a shorter run up!

I would like to thank Hugh Cushing for his wonderful sketches; Chris Beasley for his design work; Alan Heasman for the title of the book and for his hours of toil; Ana West and many other friends and family for their ideas and support; all those who have generously contributed recipes and especially Mary Butcher, the baker

Charmaine Hutton
June 1998

Cricket tea recipes - puddings & cakes

BARMOUTH BISCUITS

100g (4oz) butter or margarine
75g (3oz) sugar
115g (4 1/2oz) self-raising flour

Preheat oven to 190C, 375F or Gas Mark 5. Cream together butter and sugar. Add self-raising flour. Knead well. Roll into balls and place on greased baking tray. Press with a fork and add a cherry. Bake for 12-15 minutes until golden brown.

Mrs. D. Etchells
Kirkby-in-Furness Cricket Club, Cumbria

MARY'S CHOCOLATE CORNFLAKE CAKES

50g (2oz) butter
2 x 225g (1/2lb) bars of milk or plain chocolate, preferably Cadbury's/Bournville
250g (9oz) cornflakes

Melt butter and chocolate very slowly over a bowl of water or in the microwave. Mix in cornflakes until all are covered with the chocolate mixture. Put dessertspoonfuls into cake papers and leave to set. Makes approximately 24.

Mrs. Mary Butcher
The Cricketer, Beech Hanger, Ashurst, Kent

MISQUOTES
BY UNDERARM

It is a miracle of rare device,
This nutty cake, do try a slice.
Coleridge (on TMS)

CRICKET WHITE BROWNIES

175g (6oz) shelled hazel or other chopped nuts
500g (18oz) white chocolate
75g (3oz) butter
3 eggs, beaten
175g (6oz) caster sugar
175g (6oz) self-raising flour
Pinch of salt
5ml (1tspn) vanilla essence

Preheat oven to 190C, 375F or Gas Mark 5. Grease large rectangular baking tin. Roughly chop hazelnuts and 400g (14oz) chocolate and set aside. Melt rest of chocolate and leave to cool slightly. Cream butter and sugar and add to beaten eggs. Gradually add melted chocolate. Sift in flour and salt, then fold in mixture with chopped nuts and chocolate. Turn into baking tin and level mixture. Cook for 30-35 minutes until risen and golden. Cut into 12 'man-size' chunks.

Mrs. Kay Lawrenson
Overton-on-Dee Cricket Club, Wrexham

"Beat the eggs thoroughly . . "

ORANGE CITRUS CAKE

2 naval oranges, deseeded
1 cup ground almonds
5ml (1tspn) baking powder
1/3 cup rice flour
5 eggs
1 cup caster sugar

Syrup
Juice and finely grated rind from 2 oranges
1/2 cup of sugar

Preheat oven to 170C, 325F or Gas Mark 3. With the skin intact (making sure the seeds have been removed), roughly chop two oranges in a blender and reduce them to a paste. Combine the dry cake ingredients of ground almonds, baking powder and rice flour. Whisk the eggs together with the caster sugar for about 3 minutes, or until it is white and fluffy. Combine the dry cake ingredients, egg and caster sugar mix and orange paste. Stir gently but thoroughly. Line a spring form cake tin with baking paper, lightly greased with a little melted butter. Pour in the cake mixture and cook in the oven for 45 minutes.

To make the syrup: Combine sugar, orange juice and orange rind over heat. Allow to boil for about 3 minutes. Remove the cake from oven when cooked and pour the syrup over the cake. Allow 15 minutes for it to soak in. Serve with a dollop of thickened cream.

Ginie Bristowe
Maylands, Perth, Western Australia

"Now, you cannot make omelettes without breaking eggs, and you cannot have fast bowling without occasional knocks."

W.A Bettesworth, 1927

BRILL BREAD PUDDING

225g (8oz) stale bread
100g (4oz) currants, raisins or sultanas
50g (2oz) brown sugar
50g (2oz) finely chopped suet
25g (1oz) chopped peel
5ml (1tspn) mixed spice
1 egg
A little milk

Preheat oven to 150C, 300F or Gas Mark 2. Break the bread into small pieces and soak in cold water for at least half-an-hour. Then squeeze as dry as possible. Put into a basin and beat out the lumps with a fork. Add the dried fruit, sugar, suet, peel and mixed spice and mix well. Add the egg and enough milk to enable the mixture to drop easily from the spoon. Put into a greased tin. Bake in a warm oven for about 1 hour. When cool cut into 5 - 6 slices.

This recipe is very well-received amongst local cricketers and has the advantage of slowing down visiting fast bowlers and reducing opening batsmen in the number of quick singles that they can take!

Mrs. Maureen Jeacock
Brill Cricket Club, Buckinghamshire

ORANGE MALT TEA BREAD

2 cups sugar
2 cups dried fruit
4 cups self-raising flour
60ml (4tbspns) black treacle
1 1/2 cups milk
1 1/2 cups undiluted orange squash

Preheat oven to 170C, 325F or Gas Mark 3. Line 2 x450g (1lb) loaf tins with greaseproof paper. Mix all ingredients together until well blended. Divide mixture between tins. Bake for approximately 1 hour (test with a skewer). Serve sliced and buttered.

Mrs. Pamela M. Leaf
Walton Cricket Club, Wetherby, Yorks

PICNIC SLICES

225g (8oz) plain or milk chocolate
50g (2oz) butter
100g (4oz) caster sugar
1 egg, beaten
100g (4oz) dessicated coconut
50g (2oz) sultanas
50g (2oz) glacé cherries, chopped

Preheat oven to 150C, 300F or Gas Mark 2. Grease Swiss roll tin. Break chocolate into pieces and place in a bowl over hot water. When melted pour into bottom of tin. Leave to set. Cream the butter and sugar, then add the egg, coconut, salt and chopped cherries. Mix well and spread evenly over the chocolate. Bake for 30 minutes until golden brown. Leave to cool and cut into slices with a sharp knife.

Mrs. Joan Bowerman
Matching Green Cricket Club, Essex

MOIST FRUIT CAKE

Tray bake

450g (1lb) mixed fruit
225g (8oz) margarine
200g (7oz) sugar (white or soft brown)
250g (10oz) self-raising flour
2 eggs
1 cup water

Preheat oven to 200C, 400F or Gas Mark 6. Line an 8"x 8" square cake tin with greaseproof paper. Place fruit, margarine, sugar and water in a large saucepan. Bring to boil and leave to cool. Add flour and beaten egg. Mix well and place in the tin. Cook at 200C, 400F, Gas Mark 6 for 10 minutes then lower heat to 150C, 300F, Gas Mark 2 for 1 1/2 hours. Cool and when cold cut 3 x 8" slices. Makes 24 slices.

Mrs. J. Garley
Geddington Cricket Club, Northamptonshire

GINGERBREAD

Tray bake

675g (24oz) self-raising flour
10ml (2tspns) ground ginger
10ml (2tspns) mixed spice
340g (12oz) sugar
225g (8oz) margarine
60ml (4tbspns) black treacle
2 eggs, beaten with 2 teacups milk

Preheat oven to 165C, 320F or Gas Mark 3. Mix flour and spices. Cream margarine and sugar. Stir in treacle. Add dry ingredients and egg and milk alternately. Beat thoroughly. Fold in remaining flour. Pour into a greased and lined 12" square cake tin. Bake for 1 hour. Serve sliced.

Mrs. Mavis Tapp
Little Harrowden Cricket Club, Northamptonshire

BANANA AND ALMOND SLICE

175g (6oz) butter
175g (6oz) caster sugar
175g (6oz) self-raising flour
175g (6oz) flaked almonds
150g (5fl.oz) single cream
2 bananas, sliced

Preheat oven to 200C, 400F or Gas Mark 6. Melt butter and sugar in saucepan. Stir in flour and almonds off the heat. Take half of above and press into a greased baking dish or tin. Slice bananas over the mixture and pour on the cream. Spread the remaining ingredients on top and flatten with a knife. Bake in a hot oven until firm and golden brown. Can serve hot or cold.

Mrs. Pam Preene
Uffington Cricket Club, Oxfordshire

CHERRY, WALNUT AND MARZIPAN SANDWICH CAKE

For every 2 eggs use approximately:

100g (4oz) butter or margarine
100g (4oz) caster sugar
100g (4oz) self-raising flour
Pinch of salt
50g (2oz) cherries
50g (2oz) walnuts, chopped
15ml (1 tbspn) milk

Marzipan filling

50g (2oz) ground almonds,
50g (2oz) icing sugar
Beaten egg

Preheat oven to 150C, 300F or Gas Mark 2. Cream the butter and sugar. Add eggs, beat into creamed mixture one at a time, alternating with flour. Fold in rest of flour, cherries and nuts. Add milk last. Divide into two sandwich tins. Bake for about 40 minutes.

For the filling: Mix a little egg with the ground almonds and icing sugar. Roll out to the size of the cake and sandwich between halves.

Mrs. B. Eyre
Skellingthorpe Cricket Club, Lincolnshire

CREAM SLICES

1 pkt frozen puff pastry, thawed
Fresh whipped cream
Strawberry jam
Icing sugar

Preheat oven to 200C, 400F or Gas Mark 6. Roll out puff pastry to 1/8" thick. Cut into 3" squares and bake on a baking tray in a hot oven for 10 minutes. Cool on a wire rack. When cold split in half and fill with jam and fresh cream. Dust top with icing sugar.

Mrs. Elvina Griffiths
Carew Cricket Club, Pembrokeshire

MISQUOTES
BY UNDER ARM

"Herewith a piece of cake, beneath the bough
A cup of tea, The Cricketer and thou"
E. Fitzgerald (The Rúbaiyát of Omar Khayyám)

CHOCOLATE LUMPS

450g (1lb) digestive biscuits, crushed
200g (7oz) soft margarine or butter
45ml (3tbspns) golden syrup
30ml (2 heaped tbspns) cocoa
30ml (2tbspns) caster sugar
100g (4oz) sultanas

Put all the ingredients except the crushed biscuits and sultanas into a saucepan. Heat gently and stir frequently till butter and sugar have melted and all ingredients have combined to give a glossy smooth mixture. Mix crushed biscuits and sultanas together. Add biscuit mixture to chocolate mixture and combine well. Put into a baking tin 11"x 8". Flatten and press mixture down until it is level. Put into fridge to harden (about 4 hours). Slice into 6 pieces one way and 4 pieces the other way. Makes 24 slices.

Mrs. Patsy Webb
Falconhurst Cricket Club, Kent

SULTANA LOAF

225g (8oz) self-raising flour and a pinch of salt
225g (8oz) sultanas or dried fruit
175g (6oz) demerara sugar
175ml (6fl.oz) cold tea

Preheat oven to 180C, 350F or Gas Mark 4. Soak fruit in cold tea. Sieve flour and salt and add sugar. Mix in fruit and tea. Mix well. Put in 900g (2lb) greased loaf tin. Bake for 1 hour in the oven. When cold slice and spread with soft margarine or butter. Freezes well.

Mrs. Ann Hambrook
Winterton Cricket Club, Norfolk

AGA SHARP LEMON SLICES

Traybake

4 eggs
250g (9oz) soft margarine
250g (9oz) caster sugar
340g (12oz) self-raising flour
15ml (3 level tspns) baking powder
90ml (6tbspns) milk
Grated rind of 2 lemons

For the topping
About 75ml (5tbspns) lemon juice
340g (12oz) caster sugar

This recipe is for cooking in the Aga in a roasting tin. Measure all ingredients into a bowl and beat well for 2 minutes until smooth. Line the roasting tin with baking parchment and pour in mixture. Hang the tin on the lowest set of runners in the Aga and put the cold plain shelf on the second set of runners. Bake for about 30 minutes, turning once during cooking.

To make the topping: Warm the lemon juice and mix in the sugar. Pour over the cake whilst still warm and in the tin.

Mrs. C. M. Cox
Skellingthorpe Cricket Club, Lincolnshire

MISQUOTES
BY UNDER ARM

"Some sipping gin, some sipping tea,
But as you by their faces see
All silent and all damned."

Wordsworth.

BANANA BREAD

200g (7oz) self-raising flour sifted with
1.25ml (1/4tspn) bicarbonate of soda and 2.5ml
(1/2 tspn) salt
75g (3oz) butter or margarine
175g (6oz) caster sugar
2 eggs, beaten
450g (1lb) bananas, mashed
100g (4oz) coarsely chopped nuts

Preheat oven to 180C, 350F or Gas Mark 4. Line a 900g (2lb) loaf tin. Cream butter and sugar until pale and fluffy. Add eggs a little at a time, beating each time. Add bananas and beat. Stir in flour and nuts. Put in loaf tin and bake for 1 1/4 hours. Cut into 10-12 slices.

Mrs. B. Symons
Troon Cricket Club, Cornwall

We have been participating in the Village Championship for many years and have enjoyed the refreshments as well as the friendly competition with other village clubs.

Troon Cricket Club, Cornwall

QUICK AND EASY CHOCOLATE CAKE

250g (9oz) caster sugar
250g (9oz) soft margarine or butter
75ml (5tbspns) cocoa
90ml (6tbsns) boiling water
5 eggs
250g (9oz) self-raising flour
15ml (3tspns) baking powder

Preheat oven to 200C, 400F or Gas Mark 6. Oil baking tin approximately 12"x 10". Line base with greaseproof paper and then oil the paper. Put into food processor or food mixer the margarine, caster sugar, cocoa and boiling water. Beat well until smooth. Add eggs to mixture, also the self-raising flour to which you have added the baking powder. Beat well. Turn mixture into prepared baking tin, and smooth over the top. Put in the oven and bake for 5 minutes at 200C, 400F or Gas Mark 6. Turn oven down to 190C, 375F or Gas Mark 5 for a further 30 minutes. Remove from oven and cool. Cover with chocolate butter icing and cut 7 slices along widest side and 4 slices along other side. Makes 28 slices.

The cake keeps well in a tin if made several days in advance and freezes well.

Mrs. Patsy Webb
Falconhurst Cricket Club, Kent

TEA LADIES URGENTLY REQUIRED! Some of us are heartily sick of being shouted at from the boundary to get the kettles on!

Extract from The Griffin Cricket Team newsletter, Fletching, East Sussex

COCONUT DROPS

225g (8oz) dessicated coconut
150g (5oz) caster sugar
2 eggs, size 3
Glacé cherries

Preheat oven to 180C, 350F or Gas Mark 4. Beat eggs and add caster sugar and coconut. Place small amounts of mixture on trays, covered with baking parchment. Put half a cherry on top of each. Bake for 20-25 minutes. Makes about 20.

Mrs. Edith Barber
Hilton Cricket Club Derbyshire

CRUNCHY TOP LEMON CAKE

100g (4oz) soft margarine
175g (6oz) caster sugar
175g (6oz) self-raising flour
5ml (1tspn) baking powder
2 eggs, size 2
60ml (4tbspns) milk
Finely grated rind of 1 lemon

Crunchy Topping
Juice of 1 lemon
100g (4oz) granulated sugar

Preheat oven to 170C, 325F or Gas Mark 3. Base line a deep round sandwich tin with greaseproof paper. Measure all ingredients for the cake into a large bowl and beat well for about 2 minutes until smooth and well-blended. Turn the mixture into the prepared tin and level the surface. Bake for about 35-40 minutes until the cake has shrunk slightly from the sides of the tin and springs back when lightly pressed with a finger.

To make the crunchy topping: Measure the lemon juice and sugar into a bowl and stir until blended. When the cake comes out of the oven, spread the lemon paste over the top whilst the cake is still hot. Leave in the tin until cold, then turn out and remove paper.

Michelle Blyth
Ashurst Cricket Club, Kent

MISQUOTES
BY UNDER ARM

"Ah fill the cup - what boots it to repeat
How the game is slipping underneath our feet"
E. Fitzgerald (The Rúbaiyát of Omar Khayyám)

STICKY WICKETS

3 standard-size Mars Bars
75g (3oz) butter
75g (3oz) Rice Crispies

Topping
25g (1oz) butter
200g (7oz) milk chocolate

Chop up Mars Bars into small pieces and melt with butter VERY SLOWLY over a low heat. Stir frequently until melted. Take off heat. Stir in Rice Crispies. Put into an 8"x 8" square tin or if you want thicker pieces 6"x 6" tin.

For the topping: Melt butter and chocolate over a basin of hot water. Spread it across the tin and cool. When cool, the tin can be placed in the fridge to go hard. Cut into squares. Double quantities will spread well into a small Aga roasting tin.

Mrs. Yvonne Gerrett
Falconhurst Cricket Club, Kent

Like Raleigh flooding Britain with tobacco, Brian Johnston was responsible for slowly inundating our pokey little commentary boxes with an avalanche of cake. His plaintiff SOS for fodder when, in 1970 Nancy forgot to send up tea to our Lord's eyrie, was heard by alert cooks throughout the realm. The first offering was brought in by a lady resident of St John's Wood, one Aileen Cohen, the very next day. Once she had been warmly thanked by Johnners, the floodgates were opened to any listener craving a mention on Test Match Special. Soon anyone bearing a cake for BJ was granted a free entry, not only to our box but to the ground!

They have come in all shapes and sizes: carrot cake that smelt of wacky backy; a chocolate cricket bat that melted over Fred's jacket; a tray of concoction delivered by a lady from the Egg Marketing Board disguised as a chicken, that devoured The Boil's spectacles; a cake load of rum which our producer absentmindedly donated to the children's ward of a neighbouring hospital. Meanwhile we live in fear of some lunatic cricket-loathing chemist sending a cake with special ingredients designed to remove TMS from the airwaves!

Bill Frindall. Scorer & Statistician, BBC Test Match Special Commentary Box

WEETABIX LOAF

4 Weetabix
450g (1lb) demerara sugar
450g (1lb) mixed fruit
568ml (1 pint) milk
450g (1lb) self-raising flour
2 eggs

Soak Weetabix, sugar and mixed fruit in milk for at least 2 hours (better overnight). Mix in beaten egg and flour. Put in 2 greased 7" loaf tins. Bake slowly in the oven on 125C, 200F or Gas Mark 2 for 1 1/2 hours.

Keeps well if cricket match is cancelled.

Mrs. Brenda Till
Sessay Cricket Club, North Yorkshire

DUBLIN TEACAKE

450g (1lb) mixed fruit
100g (4oz) candied peel
100g (4oz) glacé cherries (optional)
225g (8oz) demerara sugar
1 1/2 cups cold strong tea, strained
1 egg, beaten
450g (1lb) self-raising flour

Put fruit, sugar and cold tea in a bowl and leave overnight. Next day, add 1 beaten egg and self-raising flour. Put in 2 greased 7" loaf tins. Bake in a slow oven for 1 1/2 hours.

Mrs. Margaret Flintoff (Snr.)
Sessay Cricket Club, North Yorkshire

UPSIDE-DOWN APPLE SPONGE CAKE

4 medium-sized dessert apples
30ml (2tbspns) icing sugar
15ml (1tbspn) Rum or Calvados (optional)
50g (2oz) butter, melted
115g (4 1/2 oz) caster sugar
2 eggs, size 2
100g (4oz) flour, sifted
5ml (1tspn) bicarbonate of soda
Pinch of salt

Preheat oven to 190C, 375F Or Gas Mark 5. Butter a 9" square tin. Line the tin with buttered and floured greaseproof paper. Peel, core and slice or dice the apples. Put them into a bowl, dust them with icing sugar and sprinkle with Rum or Calvados. Whisk the sugar and eggs together until they are thick and creamy. Sift the flour, bicarbonate of soda and salt together and lightly fold them into the sugar and eggs. Add the melted butter, then fold it in with the apples and their juice. Bake the cakes for 50-60 minutes or until done when tested with a fine skewer. Remove the cake from the tin. Set to cool upside-down on a rack and peel off the paper. Serve the cake upside-down, with lightly sweetened whipped or thick cream.

Mrs. Ana West
Bluemantles Cricket Club, Tunbridge Wells, Kent

CHOCOLATE FUDGE CAKE

175g (6oz) butter
75g (3oz) demerara sugar
75g (3oz) clear honey
3 eggs, beaten
115g (4 1/2oz) self-raising flour
Pinch of salt
40g (1 1/2 oz) cocoa
5ml (1tspn) dissolved instant coffee
Vanilla essence

Preheat oven to l90C, 375F or Gas Mark 5. Grease and line 2 x 7" sandwich tins or 1 x 9"x9" square tin. Cream butter, sugar and honey until light and fluffy. Add beaten eggs, a little at a time, beating well between each addition. Sieve flour, salt and cocoa together, fold into creamed mixture and add liquid coffee. Add vanilla essence and stir well. Place in prepared tins. Bake on top or middle shelf for 30 minutes until well risen.

Chocolate Fudge Icing

25g (1oz) butter or hard margarine
50g (2oz) soft brown sugar
15g (1/2 oz) cocoa mixed into a paste with 45ml (3tbspns) water
10ml (2tspns) milk
225g (8oz) icing sugar, sieved
30ml (2tbspns) water
Vanilla essence

Place the fat, sugar, liquid cocoa and milk in a saucepan and put on low heat. Stir until butter and sugar melts, bring to the boil and boil briskly for 3 minutes. Remove from the heat, add icing sugar and mix well. Add warm water, vanilla essence and beat well. Pour over cake while still warm, as this icing sets when cold.

Mrs. Eleanor Phillips
Ley Hill Cricket Club, Buckinghamshire

Unfortunately, we don't have our menfolk making teas for us-that really would be women's lib gone berserk. We solve our tea-making problem by each player bringing "tea for two"; the trouble is that we never liaise with one another, and some weeks we all bring fish paste sandwiches or another time we all bring Swiss rolls."

Rachael Heyhoe-Flint.

From The Lord's Taverners Sticky Wicket Book (Queen Anne Press)

TOSS-IN-FRUIT CAKE

225g (8oz) self-raising flour
2.5ml (1/2tspn) mixed spice
Pinch of salt
100g (4oz) soft brown sugar
300-340g (10-12oz) dried mixed fruit
2 eggs, size 3
100ml (4fl.oz) vegetable oil
100ml (4fl.oz) milk
2.5ml (1/2tspn) almond essence

Preheat oven to 130C, 250F or Gas Mark 1/2. Grease either 7" or 8" round cake tin and line base with greased paper or foil. Mix together flour, mixed spice, salt, sugar and dried fruit. Beat the eggs, cooking oil, milk and almond essence together. Add to the dry ingredients and beat thoroughly until well combined. Turn into prepared tin and sprinkle with demerara sugar. Bake for approximately 1 1/2 - 2 hours. Allow to cool in tin before turning out.

Mrs. Eleanor Phillips
Ley Hill Cricket Club, Buckinghamshire

Cakes of all sizes, colours and contents have become an integral part of Test Match Special. At a recent Test Match I devoured a slice of one which was a superb model of the new stand at Trent Bridge and much too good to eat. A dramatic moment occurred at Lord's when someone precariously placed an iced spectacular on top of our TV monitor. It slid off, but the expected disaster was prevented by Fred Trueman, who brought off a splendid one-handed catch. On another occasion, I was leaving the pavilion at Lord's for lunch when asked by a young lady if I would take a cake up to the box. However I was quickly relieved of the heavy tin by the police who were looking for an IRA bomb! Fortunately, it proved to be a false alarm. This cake bombardment has continued for three decades and has been enormous fun, even if it has been partly responsible for my putting on extra weight!

Trevor Bailey. BBC Test Match Special Commentator

COOKIES

175g (6oz) self-raising flour
175g (6oz) rolled oats
175g (6oz) sugar
175g (6oz) margarine
30ml (2 tbspns) golden syrup
5ml (1 level tspn) bicarbonate of soda
30ml (2tbspns) milk
Glacé cherries

Preheat oven to 180C, 350F or Gas Mark 4. Mix together the flour, rolled oats and sugar. In a small pan, melt margarine and golden syrup. Mix 5ml (1 tspn) bicarbonate of soda with 30ml (2 tbspns) milk and add this to oats mixture, together with melted syrup and margarine. Take teaspoonfuls of mixture, roll into a ball and place on a lightly greased baking tray - well spaced and press flat. Top with a piece of glacé cherry. Bake for about 10 minutes. Remove from tray immediately when cooked.

Town Street Ladies
Carlton Cricket Club, Yorkshire

A father gave the following credentials for his son. "He has put up the numbers on the telegraph since the age of nine; played for the under 15's since the age of eleven; played for the 1st XI since the age of fourteen; and if that's not enough, I can tell you, as his father, that he was conceived after tea in the back of the pavilion!

Ben Brocklehurst, Chairman
The Cricketer, Beech Hanger, Ashurst, Kent.

MICROWAVE LEMON CAKE

175g (6oz) butter or margarine
175g (6oz) soft brown sugar
175g (6oz) self-raising flour
3 eggs, size 2, lightly beaten
Grated rind of 1 lemon

Topping
Juice of 1 lemon
4oz caster sugar

Recipe is for Microwave 650 watts. Melt fat and sugar together in a pan. Beat in flour, eggs and lemon rind. Pour into greased microwave dish. Cook on full power for 3 1/2 minutes until cake is just dry on surface and pulling away from side of dish. Adjust cooking time to suit your microwave. Mix lemon juice and caster sugar and pour over the cake. When cold the topping will go crunchy.

Mrs. Beryl Richardson
Moorsholm Cricket Club, North Yorkshire

MISQUOTES
BY UNDERARM

"The ball no question makes of Ayes and Noes.
But here or there as strikes the player goes;
And he that knocked you all about the field.
Only for tea his wicket yields."

E. Fitzgerald (The Rubáiyát of Omar Khayyám)

SCONES

225g (8oz) self-raising flour, sifted
10ml (2tspns) baking powder, sifted
50g (2oz) butter or margarine
25g (1oz) caster sugar
1 egg
Milk

Preheat oven to 220C, 425F or Gas Mark 7. Lightly grease 2 baking trays. Measure the flour and baking powder into a bowl, then add the fat and rub in with the fingertips until the mixture resembles fine breadcrumbs. Stir in the sugar. Break the egg into a measuring jug, then make up to 150ml (5fl.oz) with milk. Stir the egg and milk into the flour, (you may not need it all), and mix to a soft but not sticky dough. Turn out onto a lightly floured work surface. Knead lightly and then roll out to a thickness of 1/2". Cut into rounds with a fluted 2" cutter and place them on the prepared baking trays. Brush the tops with a little extra milk, or any egg and milk left over in the jug. Bake in the oven for about 10 minutes or until scones are a pale golden brown. Lift on to a wire rack to cool. Eat as fresh as possible - but can be frozen and reheated.

Makes 10-12.

Michelle Blyth
Ashurst Cricket Club, Kent

A member at Hartley Country Club in Kent took his guests, a family of four and all French, to see their very first cricket match. The weather was good, the company congenial and to his relief his guests seemed well entertained. Then over tea, Madame remarked "This is very charming, cher Colin, but tell me please, when does the game begin?"

Recalled by Hugh Cushing (of Colin Senneck)

ANZAC BISCUITS

100g (4oz) margarine
30ml (2tbspns) golden syrup
1 cup self-raising flour
1 cup porridge oats
1 cup dessicated coconut
1 cup brown sugar
5ml (1tspn) bicarbonate of soda

Preheat oven to 180C, 350F or Gas Mark 4. Grease a baking tray covered with baking parchment. In a saucepan, melt margarine and syrup. Meanwhile in a large bowl, mix all other ingredients. When melted, mix the margarine and syrup with the dry ingredients and stir well. Roll the mixture into small balls and place on baking tray. Cook for 20 minutes until golden brown. Remove from oven and cool. When cold each biscuit can be dipped in melted chocolate (if desired). A cup of muesli can be used as an alternative to the coconut.

Makes 20-25.

Mrs. Jan Orchard
Cornwood Cricket Club, Devon

GINGERBREAD CAKE

Traybake

284ml (1/2pint) milk
225g (8oz) margarine
30ml (2tbspns) golden syrup
30ml (2tbspns) treacle

450g (1lb) self-raising flour
225g (8oz) caster sugar
20ml (4tspns) ground ginger
10ml (2tspns) mixed spice
Pinch of salt
1 egg, beaten
5ml (1tspn) bicarbonate of soda

Preheat oven to 180C, 350F or Gas Mark 4. Place milk, margarine and golden syrup and treacle in a pan. Stir and warm until the ingredients are mixed. Do not boil. Pour this on to the dry ingredients. Add a beaten egg and mix well. Dissolve 10ml (2tspns) bicarbonate of soda in 30ml (2tbspns) of milk. Add this and mix well. Line a square roasting tin with greaseproof paper and pour in mixture. Bake in oven for 45 minutes or when pricked with skewer it will come out clean. Store in tin for a few days before using.

This recipe is extremely moist and a great favourite. It has won prizes at Horticultural shows!

Mrs. M. B. Jacques
Shireshead and Forton Cricket Club, Lancashire

SHORTBREAD

350g (12 1/2oz) plain flour
65g (2 1/2oz) ground rice
150g (5oz) caster sugar
300g (10oz) butter or block margarine

Preheat oven to 150C, 300F or Gas Mark 2. Sift flour, salt and ground rice into bowl. Add sugar and grate butter taken straight from fridge into dry ingredients. Work mixture well with fingertips until it resembles breadcrumbs. Press mixture into a greased Swiss roll tin and level the top. Prick all over with a fork and mark into equal portions cutting right through to base of tin. Chill in fridge. Bake for about 1 hour until pale golden colour. Cool in tin before putting on wire rack.

Mrs. Andrea Brocklehurst
Falconhurst Cricket Club, Kent

BARER BREATH

175g (6oz) self-raising flour
100g (4oz) demerara sugar
100g (4oz) mixed fruit
1 egg
1 cup black tea
15ml (1tbspn) marmalade

Soak tea, fruit and sugar overnight. Preheat oven to 200C, 400F or Gas Mark 6. Add egg and marmalade to the mixture. Mix in the flour. Place in a 450g (1lb) greased loaf tin and cook for I hour. Cut into slices and butter.

Mrs. Avril Goss
Halkyn Cricket Club, Flintshire

BANANA LOAF

225g (8oz) self-raising flour
100g (4oz) margarine
100g (4oz) sugar
2 eggs
2 bananas

Preheat oven to 190C, 375F or Gas Mark 5. Mash bananas in a dish. Cream margarine and sugar and gradually add beaten eggs. Add mashed banana and fold in flour. Place in a greased loaf tin and cook for 30 minutes. Slice when cold.

Mrs. Avril Goss
Halkyn Cricket Club, Flintshire

BAKEWELL TART

75g (3oz) flour
75g (3oz) margarine
50g (2oz) sugar
1 egg
5ml (1 tspn) almond essence
Shortcrust pastry
Jam
Glaze icing

Preheat oven to 160C, 330F or Gas Mark 3. Line greased 7" tin with pastry. Spread thin layer of jam on top. Place all ingredients (except icing) into a bowl, mix until smooth and pour into the pastry case. Bake for 20 minutes. Leave to cool. Make glaze icing. Spread on top.

Mrs. Linda Ivey
Newdigate Cricket Club, Surrey

MISQUOTES
BY UNDERARM

Six players in search of a tea tent
Pirandello

COFFEE AND WALNUT SPONGE

225g (8oz) soft tub margarine
225g (8oz) caster sugar
225g (8oz) self-raising flour
4 eggs
15ml (1tbspn) coffee essence

Filling

275g (10oz) icing sugar
150g (5oz) butter
15ml (1 level tbspn) coffee powder
A little hot water

Preheat oven to 180-190C, 350-375F or Gas Mark 4-5. Place all ingredients in food processor bowl and process until smooth, or place into a mixing bowl and beat for 2 minutes. Divide between 2 greased and floured 8" or 9" sandwich tins and bake for approximately 25-30 minutes above centre of oven until cake springs back when lightly pressed. Turn out carefully onto a wire rack to cool.

To make the filling: Put the butter in a bowl and cream until soft. Gradually beat in the sifted icing sugar. Blend 15ml (1 level tbspn) coffee powder with the water to give a smooth paste. Add to the butter and icing sugar and beat until a fluffy consistency. Sandwich cakes together with the filling and top with remaining icing. Decorate top with chopped or whole walnuts.

Mrs. Anne Roberts
Enville Cricket Club, Stourbridge, West Midlands

CARAMEL SHORTCAKE

Shortcake

100g (4oz) block margarine or butter
75g (3oz) caster sugar
225g (8oz) plain flour

Caramel

100g (4oz) block margarine or butter
100g (4oz) caster sugar
30ml (2tbspns) golden syrup
1 small tin condensed milk

Topping

150g (5oz) cooking chocolate

Preheat oven to 180C, 350F or Gas Mark 4. Grease a Swiss roll tin.

To make shortcake: Cream the fat and sugar. Sift the flour and stir into the creamed mixture. Press the mixture into the tin until firm. Bake for 15-20 minutes until firm to touch and pale brown in colour.

To make the caramel: Place all ingredients in a pan and melt. Stir all the time on a low heat until it thickens and turns golden brown. Pour over the shortcake, leave to cool.

To make the topping: Melt the chocolate, then pour over the caramel. Cut into fingers or squares.

Mrs. Barbara Macdonald
Bates Cottages Cricket Club, Northumberland

MISQUOTES
BY UNDER ARM

"Let them eat cake"

Marie Antoinette (heard on TMS)

CHOCOLATE BROWNIES

85g (3 3/4oz) butter or block margarine
75g (3oz) chocolate
250g (9oz) caster sugar
85g (3 3/4oz) self-raising flour
3 eggs
Pinch of salt
3.75ml (3/4tspn) vanilla essence
75g (3oz) walnuts (optional)

Preheat oven to 180C, 350F or Gas Mark 4. Grease and flour 12" Swiss roll tin. Melt chocolate and butter very slowly. Add sugar. Sift flour with salt into a bowl. Stir in chocolate mixture and beaten eggs and vanilla (and optional walnuts). Beat till smooth and spoon into tin. Bake for 35 minutes till mixture is risen and leaves sides of tin. Leave to cool before cutting into 2" squares. Makes 24-30.

Mrs. Andrea Brocklehurst
Falconhurst Cricket Club, Kent

Henry Blofeld, BBC Test Match Special Commentator

"A large brown éclair goes down the Kennington Road . . ."

CARROT AND WALNUT CAKE

225g (8oz) plain flour
400g (14oz) soft brown sugar
340ml (12fl.oz) vegetable oil
4 eggs
400g (14oz) carrots, grated
300g (10oz) walnuts, chopped
10ml (2tspns) bicarbonate soda
5ml (1tspn) cinnamon
2.5ml (1/2tspn) salt
Pinch of nutmeg

Frosting

100g (4oz) cream cheese
40g (1 1/2oz) butter
100g (4oz) castor sugar
3 drops vanilla essence
1 tin chopped pineapple, drained

Preheat oven to 180C, 350F or Gas Mark 4. Grease and base line a 7" square cake tin. Sift the flour, bicarbonate of soda, cinnamon, nutmeg and salt together in a large bowl. Mix the sugar and oil together in another bowl, then add the eggs. Make a well in the flour, and stir in the liquid, then the carrots and walnuts. Spoon the cake mixture into tin and bake for between 2 - 2 1/2 hours. Leave the cake to cool in the tin, then turn out onto a wire rack. When cold, wrap in foil and leave for a day.

To make the frosting: Mash the cream cheese, butter, sugar and vanilla essence together, then stir in the well-drained pineapple. Spread over the top of the cake and serve cut into squares.

Mrs. C. J. Bilton
Woodhouse Grange Cricket Club, Yorkshire

JAMAICAN TARTS

Filling

225g (8oz) Golden Delicious apples, peeled and diced
2 bananas
50g (2oz) crystalized ginger, pared very finely
2.5ml (1/2tspn) ground ginger
20ml (4 rounded tspns) orange marmalade
25g (1oz) butter
50g (2oz) sugar
20ml (1 1/2tbspns) Rum

Melt butter and sugar in a saucepan and add all the other ingredients. Cook until mixture has thickened and apples are soft and mushy. Remove from heat and cool. Mix in rum.

To make Button Meringues: Use 2 egg whites and 100g (4oz) caster sugar. Whisk ingredients in a bowl which has been placed over gently simmering water. When mixture has thickened remove from heat and carry on beating until stiff glossy peaks have formed. Be careful not to allow meringue to become too warm. Dot teaspoonfuls of mixture onto flat trays covered with baking parchment and bake for 1-1 1/2 hours until crisp in oven on 120C, 230F, Gas Mark 1/2.

To make 24 vol-au-vent cases: Take 2 packs of frozen puff pastry (or use home-made). Roll out thawed pastry to 1/4" thick and cut 24 circles using 2 1/2" cutter. Using 1 1/2" cutter make indentation into each round to roughly half-way through its thickness. Bake in very a hot oven at 230C, 450F or Gas Mark 8 for 12 minutes. When cool scoop out thc indentations.

To assemble: Put 1 teaspoon of filling topped by 5ml (1tspn) whipped double cream into each vol-au-vent case. Just before serving pop a button meringue on each tart.

Mrs. Mavis Wingrove
Fletching Cricket Club, East Sussex

BETTY'S WELSH CAKES

450g (1lb) self-raising flour
5ml (1tspn) salt
2.5ml (1/2tspn) mixed spice
225g (8oz) lard or margarine
225g (8oz) caster sugar
100g (4oz) currants or sultanas
2 large eggs, lightly beaten
A little milk
Cooking time - 10 minutes

Sieve together the flour, salt and mixed spice. Rub in the lard or margarine until mixture resembles fine bread crumbs. Add the sugar and currants or sultanas. Stir in the beaten egg and mix to a stiff dough, adding a little milk, if necessary. Place on a floured surface, knead lightly and roll out to 1/4" thick. Cut into rounds with a 2 1/2" pastry cutter. Thoroughly grease a griddle or thick frying pan and heat, testing the temperature so that the dough browns in about 5 minutes or until evenly browned. Turn over with a palette knife and cook for 5 minutes on the other side.

Mrs Betty Shipperley
Brill Cricket Club, Buckinghamshire

The system we adopt at Ley Hill CC is to select a player to provide the tea. How he chooses to do it is up to him. One member provided a Lyons' sponge cake and a bottle of whisky!

Ley Hill Cricket Club, Buckinghamshire

CARROT CAKE

60g (2 1/2oz) moist dark brown sugar
2 eggs
175ml (6fl.oz) vegetable oil
3.75ml (3/4 tspn) salt
100g (4oz) plain flour, sifted
5ml (1tspn) bicarbonate of soda
5ml (1tspn) ground cinnamon
2 large carrots, peeled and coarsely grated
75g (3oz) walnuts or pecans, chopped
5ml (1tspn) orange rind, grated
5ml (1tspn) lemon rind, grated

<u>Cream cheese icing</u>
100g (4oz) cream cheese, softened
40g (1 1/2oz) butter or soft margarine
2.5ml (1/2 tspn) vanilla essence
175g (6oz) icing sugar, sifted

Preheat oven to 180C, 350F or Gas Mark 4. Grease and line a 9" round cake tin. Place the sugar, eggs and oil into a mixing bowl and beat well (2 minutes with an electric mixer). In a small bowl, combine the salt, flour, bicarbonate of soda and cinnamon, add to the sugar mixture. Beat slowly for 1 minute, then fold in the carrots, walnuts, orange and lemon rind. Pour batter into a tin and spread evenly. Bake for 30 minutes or until a metal skewer inserted into the centre of the cake comes out clean. Cool in the tin on a wire rack for 10 minutes, then turn out. Allow to cool before decorating with cream cheese icing.

To make the icing: In a mixing bowl beat the cream cheese, butter and vanilla essence until smooth. Gradually beat in the sugar until well blended. Spread over the top and sides of the cake as desired.

Tip : This recipe can be used to make an apple cake, by substituting 2 large apples, cored and grated - for the carrots.

Mrs. Beryl Holt
Pontblyddyn Cricket Club, Flintshire

At Halkyn cricket's not a bore -
We've pranksters, jokers, plonkers and more.
So 'Lads' this poem's to show that I care.
Even though our club has more than its share.

But better sportsmen and gentlemen you'll never find,
I've trained them well, bear that in mind.
I get great pleasure - in return -
For empty plates and an empty urn.

There must be something in it for me,
For each season to return, I agree,
Sausage rolls, butties, salads, crisps and cake,
Ice cream, fruit, jellies and biscuits I make.

From 'My place' in the kitchen,
I can see through the hatch
How well the 'lads' are doing
And who made which catch.

To sum up my thoughts
When it's all down to me,
There's no other club
Where I'd rather be!

Avril Goss. Halkyn Cricket Club, Flintshire

HOME-MADE FRUIT CAKE

450g (1lb) self-raising flour
225g (8oz) margarine
225g (8oz) caster or dark brown sugar
6 eggs
5ml (1tspn) mixed spice (optional)
1/2 cup currants
1/2 cup sultanas
1/2 cup raisins
1/4 cup peel
1/2 cup nuts
1/2 cup cherries
A few drops of almond essence

Preheat oven to 200C, 400F or Gas Mark 6. Cream margarine and sugar. Add eggs one at a time to make a creamy mixture. Add flour, a little at a time and fruit. Mix well together. Place in a large greased and lined 9" cake tin and bake for 1/2 hour on 200C, 400F or Gas Mark 6 and then turn down to 130C, 250F or Gas Mark 1/2 for a further 1 1/2 hours.

Take care not to dry cake out by overcooking.

Mrs. M. R. Gead
Boconnoc Cricket Club, Cornwall

A rural cricket match in buttercup time, seen and heard through the trees; it is surely the loveliest scene in England and the most disarming sound. From the ranks of the unseen dead forever passing along our country lanes on their eternal journey, the Englishmen fall out for a moment to look over the gate of the cricket field and smile.

Sir James Barrie

NUTTY FLAPJACK

225g (8oz) margarine
100g (4oz) self-raising flour
30ml (2tbspns) golden syrup
225g (8oz) sugar
175g (6oz) crushed cornflakes
100g (4oz) oats

Preheat oven to 190C, 375F or Gas Mark 5. Melt margarine and syrup in pan. Do not overheat. Mix in a bowl sugar, oats, flour and cornflakes. Pour the margarine mixture on dry ingredients and mix thoroughly. Place in a well-greased large baking tin for 20 minutes until firm. Cut into slices whilst still hot. Leave in tin to cool. Makes 26-30 fingers.

Mrs. Joyce Harding
Moorsholm Cricket Club, North Yorkshire

One-upmanship at the Staggerers

LEMON CURD

4 lemons
700g (1 1/2lb) sugar
8 eggs, beaten
225g (1/2lb) butter

Melt the sugar and butter. Squeeze the lemons and add the juice with the beaten eggs to the melted sugar and butter. Stir over a simmering heat until it thickens. Makes 4 x 1lb jars.

Use to fill Victoria sponge cakes and tarts.

Mrs. D. Porter
Skellingthorpe Cricket Club, Lincolnshire

All the players bring tea for two! This ensures an excellent variety of teas, as all players try to out-do each other. The sandwiches are always a brilliant selection and there are also several different cakes.

The Staggerers Cricket Club, Andover, Hampshire

PIKELETS

450g (1lb) self-raising flour
10ml (2tspns) cream of tartar
5ml (1tspn) bicarbonate of soda
100g (4oz) sugar
568ml (1pint)

Sieve flour, cream of tartar and bicarbonate of soda. Stir in sugar. Add eggs and gradually add milk, taking out all lumps. Beat until mixture is like thick batter and air bubbles appear on the surface. Grease a hot griddle, heavy frying pan or top of Rayburn. Drop large spoonfuls of batter onto the griddle a few inches apart. When bubbles appear, turn over and cook for a few seconds more. Put onto a warm plate and keep covered with a clean tea towel until cool. Serve buttered or toasted and top with syrup. Will freeze well.

Mrs. Elvina Griffiths.
Carew Cricket Club, Pembrokeshire

We had a "wet behind the ears" tea lady who responded with regal waves of the hand to the players who were waving frantically at her, in what she took to be appreciation at the tea she had just produced for them. In fact she had just driven her car straight across the sacred ground!

Mrs Mavis E. Wingrove. Fletching Cricket Club

GINGER PARKIN

225g (8oz) self-raising flour
100g (4oz) margarine
100g (4oz) brown soft sugar
5ml (1tspn) ground ginger
2.5ml (1/2tspn) bicarbonate soda
30ml (2tbspns) golden syrup
1 cup milk, boiled

Preheat oven to 200C, 400F or Gas Mark 6. Rub margarine into flour, and add all other ingredients. Boil milk and add to mixture. Mix well (mixture will be very runny). Bake in oven for 30-40 minutes in a flat Swiss roll tin, not loaf tin. Cut into squares. Freezes well.

Mrs. Beryl Richardson
Moorsholm Cricket Club, North Yorkshire

LOWDHAM FLAPJACK

250g (9oz) margarine
175g (6oz) caster sugar
250g (9oz) rolled porridge oats
75g (3oz) self-raising flour
30ml (2tbspns) golden syrup
Pinch of salt

Preheat oven to 190C, 375F or Gas Mark 5. Brush a 12"x 8" Swiss roll tin with a little melted fat. Melt margarine and syrup in a pan over low heat. Stir in the sugar and mix well. Stir in the oats and sifted flour and salt. Place mixture in a greased Swiss roll tin. Bake on the centre shelf for approximately 20 minutes until light golden brown. Cut into 16 fingers and leave to cool. Transfer to a wire tray and store in a tin.

Rebecca Seager
Lowdham Cricket Club, Nottinghamshire

CHOCOLATE CAKE

200g (7oz) self-raising flour
225g (8oz) caster sugar
2.5ml (1/2tspn) salt
15ml (1tbspn) cocoa
100g (4oz) margarine
2 eggs
75ml (5tbspns) evaporated milk
75ml (5tbspns) water
Few drops of vanilla essence

Icing

65g (2 1/2oz) margarine
25g (1oz) cocoa
250g (9oz) sieved icing sugar
45ml (3tbspns) hot milk
5ml (1tspn) vanilla essence

Preheat oven to 180C, 350F or Gas Mark 4. Grease and flour 2 firm-based 8" sandwich tins (if the bases are loose the mixture may run out). Sieve flour and cocoa, then add sugar. Rub in margarine. Beat eggs with evaporated milk then stir in vanilla essence and water. Divide mixture between tins. Bake for 30-35 minutes.

To make icing: Melt margarine. Blend in cocoa and then sieved icing sugar, milk and vanilla essence. Beat until thick and smooth. Cover and fill the cake.

Mrs. K. Milburn
Kirkby-in-Furness Cricket Club, Cumbria

The Englishman's interest in cricket springs, I believe, from a devotion to the game's simplicity bred in the English countryside - and , even at the highest level, he wishes this basic virtue to be apparent.

S.C. Griffith. Sussex and England, 1963

PASSION CAKE

175g (6oz) self-raising wholemeal flour
175g (6oz) caster sugar
175g (6oz) butter
3 eggs, beaten
2 raw carrots, grated
15ml (1tbspn) golden syrup
15ml (1tbspn) water
45ml (3tbspns) walnuts

Icing

275g (10oz) cream cheese (full fat)
100g (4oz) icing sugar
15ml (1tbspn) lemon juice

Preheat oven to 180C, 350F or Gas Mark 4. Cream together the butter and sugar until light and fluffy. Add the eggs and water a little at a time, beating well after each addition. Lightly fold in the flour and carrots. Add the golden syrup and walnuts. Divide mixture between 2 x greased 7" cake tins. Cook at the top of the oven for 25-35 minutes until the cake is risen and golden brown. Turn out of tins and cool on a wire tray.

To make the icing: Mix the cream cheese, icing sugar and lemon juice together and beat till smooth. Sandwich the 2 halves with the mixture and then spread the rest on top of the cake and decorate with walnuts.

Mrs. I.M. Smith
Hathersage Cricket Club, Yorkshire

SUSIE'S PERFECT MERINGUES

4 large egg whites
225g (8oz) caster sugar or soft brown sugar
Electric mixer with large open bowl (not a food processor)

Preheat oven to 150C, 300F or Gas Mark 2. Line a baking sheet with foil - dull side up. Put egg whites into mixer and whisk on high speed until stiff and peaky. Add sugar in 4 bursts, whilst mixer is still on high speed, allowing each burst of sugar to be incorporated before adding the next. Using a large metal spoon, gently fill a large piping bag (with a large potato star nozzle) with meringue mix and pipe on to a baking sheet. Place in the oven, turn heat down to 100C and bake to dry out for about 7 hours or overnight. Peel meringues gently off the foil and serve sandwiched with thick double cream. Makes approximately 24.

Mrs. Susan Wells
Groombridge, East Sussex

Paul Allott, Sky TV Commentator
"Cakes, cakes, cakes! It's all pie in the sky to me"

FRUIT SCONES

450g (1lb) self-raising flour
75g (3oz) lard
50g (2oz) sugar
100g (4oz) currants or sultanas
2 eggs, beaten (put aside 15ml (1tbspn) for glaze)
Milk (to make a soft dough)
5ml (1tspn) salt

Preheat oven to 200C, 400F or Gas Mark 6. Mix flour and salt in basin. Rub in lard and mix in sugar and fruit. Stir in beaten eggs and sufficient milk to make a dough. Roll out to 1/2" thickness and cut into rounds using a 2 1/2" scone cutter. Place on greased baking tray. Brush over with beaten egg. Bake in the oven for about 10 minutes. Makes 28 scones.

Mrs. D. Gillett
Thorpe Arnold Cricket Club, Leicestershire

TOFFEE CRISPS

200g (7oz) Marshmallows
100g (4oz) slab toffee
100g (4oz) butter
175g (6oz) Rice Crispies

Melt toffee, marshmallows and butter over gentle heat. Stir in Rice Crispies. Put in a greased square tin. When cool slice into squares.

Mrs. Jackie Mills
Ashurst Cricket Club, Kent

CHERRY CAKE

225g (8oz) self-raising flour
175g (6oz) cherries cut into quarters
100g (4oz) sugar
100g (4oz) margarine
2 eggs, beaten with 60ml (4tbspns) milk
12 drops of vanilla essence

Preheat oven to 180-190C, 350-375F or Gas Mark 4-5. Mix flour and quartered cherries. Beat sugar and margarine to a cream. Stir in beaten liquids and flour alternately, a little at a time. Mix thoroughly. Use a well-greased 6" cake tin, 2" deep. Bake for 1 1/4 hours, or until a skewer comes out clean.

Mrs. D. Gillett
Thorpe Arnold Cricket Club, Leicestershire

APPLE AND SULTANA CAKE

340g (12oz) self-raising flour
225g (8oz) butter or margarine
175g (6oz) sugar
100g (4oz) sultanas
3 eggs
450g (1lb) cooking apples, grated

Preheat oven to 180C, 350F or Gas Mark 4. Rub fat into the flour. Add sugar, sultanas and grated apples. Mix in the beaten eggs. Place mixture in lined and greased 8" tin, square or round. Sprinkle top with granulated or brown sugar for a crunchy topping. Cook for 1.20 to 1.30 hours. Allow to cool for 10 minutes before removing from tin and place on a rack until cold. Serves 12.

Mrs. Mary Butcher
The Cricketer, Beech Hanger, Ashurst, Kent

KIWI AND STRAWBERRY GÂTEAU

225g (8oz) butter
225g (8oz) caster sugar
225g (8oz) self-raising flour
4 eggs, medium
10ml (2tspns) baking powder
Fresh whipped cream
Fresh strawberries
Kiwi fruit

Preheat oven to 180C, 350F or Gas Mark 4. Grease and line 2 x 8" deep cake tins. Put all cake ingredients into a bowl except the fruit and cream. Beat together until smooth and light for 1-2 minutes with an electric mixer. Pour into cake tins. Bake in centre of oven for approximately 30-40 minutes. Cool. Divide each cake into 3 and layer with fresh cream and sliced kiwi fruit and strawberries. Dust icing sugar on top of cake and decorate with sliced fruit. Makes 2 cakes.

Mrs. Anne Freeman, Little Harrowden Cricket Club, Northamptonshire

Twenty-two men were soon hard at work in the homely pavilion. Some of them ate more sandwiches than they'd scored runs.

Nico Craven from "Tea for Twenty-Two", 1983

NEW ZEALAND SUMMER BERRY PAVLOVA WITH RASPBERRY COULIS

4 egg whites
60ml (4tbspns) cold water
225g (8oz) caster sugar
10ml (1dsspn) cornflour
5ml (1tspn) vanilla essence
5ml (1tspn) vinegar
Raspberries for decoration

Coulis
500g (1lb 2oz) raspberries
Icing sugar to taste

Preheat oven to 200C, 400F or Gas Mark 6. Beat egg whites and cold water until stiff. Add remaining ingredients and beat well. Pour onto a greased tray and shape into a round (cake) mould. Cook for 30 minutes and leave in the oven overnight so it does not fall.

To make the coulis: Purée the raspberries in a blender, then push through a nylon seive to remove the seeds. Add icing sugar to taste. Makes 1/2 litre (1 pint)

To serve, pile with whipped double cream and raspberries then slice and drizzle with raspberry sauce.

Georgie Murfitt
The Willows Cricket Club, Loburn, North Canterbury, New Zealand

MISQUOTES
BY UNDERARM

Come you back to the pavilion
Where the sandwiches are made
Can't you hear the cups a-clinkin'
Where the tables are all laid?

Kipling (Mandalay)

WALNUT BREAD

275g (10oz) plain flour
100g (4oz) margarine
250g (9oz) sugar
4 eggs
10ml (2tspns) baking powder
5ml (1tspn) vanilla essence
50g (2oz) walnuts
142ml (1/4pint) milk
1.25ml (1/4tspn) salt
Apricot jam

Preheat oven to 180C, 350F or Gas Mark 4. Cream margarine and sugar. Add eggs and beat well. Add flour, salt and baking powder. Drop vanilla essence into milk and mix into the dry ingredients. Put into a greased loaf tin. Bake for 20 minutes. When cool cut into slices and spread with apricot jam.

Mrs. June Farnaby
Cayton Cricket Club, North Yorkshire

Fred Trueman, BBC Test Match Special Commentator
"I don't know what's going off up here - I just don't understand it at all - who's eaten all the cake?"

"Everyone loves village cricket. Whatever your level, whether you be club cricketer or Test cricketer-or even no cricketer at all-you will find something quite irresistible about the game on the village green. In a bustle of activity attack is the keynote. No time to push or prod. The match has to be won and lost before the sun goes down-to be relived over and over again at the hostelry close by."

The Lord Cowdrey of Tonbridge, Kent and England

Cricket tea recipes - savouries, lunches & dinners

"A dangerous meal, lunch. I have known men bowl like angels before it, and roll onto the field like gorged pythons afterwards.

N.A.Knox, Surrey, 1907

CHEESE SCONES

175g (6oz) self-raising flour
25g (1oz) butter
75g (3oz) grated Cheddar cheese
2.5ml (1/2tspn) dry mustard
1 egg
60ml (4tbspns) milk
Salt and pepper

Preheat oven to 220C, 425F or Gas Mark 7. Rub butter into flour. Mix in half the cheese, salt, pepper and mustard. Mix egg with 2 tablespoons of milk. Add to mixture to make light dough. Add more milk if necessary. Roll out to 1/2" in thickness. Cut into rounds and brush tops with milk and sprinkle with remaining cheese. Bake for 15 minutes until golden brown.

Mrs. Mary Brown
Matching Green Cricket Club, Essex

Communications with the boundary . . .

'One lump for me . ."

CHEESE LOAF

75g (3oz) margarine
225g (8oz) self-raising flour
5ml (1 level tspn) baking powder
5ml (1 level tspn) dry mustard
2.5ml (1/2tspn) salt
1.25ml (1/4tspn) pepper
4 rashers bacon, rind removed and chopped
1 egg, medium
75g (3oz) Cheddar cheese, grated
150ml (1/4pint) milk
Chopped chives (optional)

Preheat oven to 190C, 375F or Gas Mark 5. Line a 450g (1lb) deep loaf tin with greaseproof paper and brush sides and base with melted butter. Sieve together the dry ingredients and place with remainder of ingredients into a mixing bowl. Beat together with a wooden spoon until well mixed (2-3 minutes). Place the mixture in the tin and bake for 40-45 minutes. Remove from the oven and leave in the tin for 5 minutes before turning out. When cold, slice and spread with butter.

Mrs. Jackie Nicholls
Matching Green Cricket Club, Essex

"I'll take two! . "

CHEESE AND ONION QUICHE

Pastry

175g (6oz) self-raising flour
40g (1 1/2oz) block margarine
40g (1 1/2oz) lard
Pinch of salt

Filling

2 onions
2 eggs
100ml (4 fl.oz) milk
100g (4oz) matured Cheddar cheese, grated
Salt & pepper

Preheat oven to 180C, 350F or Gas Mark 4. Rub the fat into flour with salt. Place the pastry into the fridge to rest for 1/2 hour. Meantime, cut onions with a knob of butter. Place the onions in a microwave for about 3 minutes or sweat in a frying pan until softened. Roll out the pastry. Place onions in the pie dish on top of the pastry. Sprinkle grated cheese on the onions. Beat the eggs and milk together. Pour over the onions and cheese and cook for approximately 30-40 minutes.

Mrs. Margaret Clayton,
Enville Cricket Club, Stourbridge, West Midlands

At our Club, we don't put the names of the ladies on the tea rota but the names of the men. Albeit it is the wives, girlfriends, daughters etc. who actually do the majority of the work. However, on occasions, it has been known for the opposite gender to be seen with a teapot or tea towel in hand!

Hartley Country Club, Kent

CHEESE STRAWS

100g (4oz) plain flour
75g (3oz) butter, at room temperature
50g (2oz) mature Cheddar cheese, grated
1 egg yolk, size 1
Finely grated Parmesan cheese for sprinkling

Lightly grease 2 baking trays. Measure the flour into a bowl and rub in the butter until the mixture resembles fine breadcrumbs. Stir in the grated Cheddar cheese. Reserve a small amount of egg yolk for glazing and stir in the remainder. Bring the mixture together to form a pastry. Wrap in cling film and chill in the fridge for about 30 minutes.

Preheat the oven to 190C, 375F or Gas Mark 5. Roll the chilled dough out on a lightly floured work surface to a thickness of about 1/4". Cut into neat strips about 1/4" wide and about 4" long. Place on the prepared baking trays. Brush with the remaining egg yolk and sprinkle generously with grated Parmesan. Bake in oven for about 10-15 minutes or until golden. Lift off the baking trays and allow to cool completely on a wire rack. Makes 30.

Michelle Blyth
Ashurst Cricket Club, Kent

SAUSAGE PARCELS

450g (1lb) pork sausagemeat
450g (1lb) shortcrust pastry
1 small tin mixed vegetables
1 medium onion, chopped
Pinch of mixed herbs
1 egg, beaten
Salt and pepper

Preheat oven to 200C, 400F or Gas Mark 6. Roll out shortcrust pastry and cut into 3" squares. Mix together the sausagemeat, mixed vegetables, herbs, onion, salt and pepper. Place a dessertspoonful of sausagemeat mixture into the centre of the pastry. Dampen 2 alternate corners with water and bring together pinching firmly. Brush top with egg and milk and bake for approximately 40 minutes until golden brown.

Mrs. M. Pawlett
St. Ishmael's Sports and Social Club, Pembrokeshire

If women want to shed the perennial tea-making role they could try persuading the men it should be replaced by a barbecue - a form of cuisine all men seem to think is their strict prerogative.

Hugh Cushing

NEW ZEALAND WHITEBAIT FRITTERS

2 cups whitebait
4 eggs
60ml (4tbspns) flour
5ml (1tspn) salt
60ml (4tbspns) oil

In a medium bowl, whisk the eggs until frothy. Fold in the flour and salt. Add the whitebait and stir to combine. Heat the butter and oil in a frying pan. Drop spoonfuls of whitebait batter into hot butter. When golden brown, turn over to cook on the other side. Serve with lemon wedges, parsley and salad. Serves 12.

Georgie Murfitt
The Willows Cricket Club, Loburn, North Canterbury, New Zealand

A recently married member asked his brand-new wife to prepare teas for the first time and he told her that the cricketers always had fillings such as Marmite and banana or peanut butter instead of the more traditional ham, cheese or egg. So that is what she did. Relations between husband and wife were rather strained for a time!

Ley Hill Cricket Club, Buckinghamshire

OUTBACK PIE

50g (2oz) butter
225g (8oz) finely chopped ham
900g (2lb) minced beef
4 medium-sized carrots, finely chopped
450g (8oz) field mushrooms, finely chopped
450g (1lb) green peas
900g (2lb) potatoes
2 onions
1/2 cup beef stock
1/2 cup gravy
15ml (1tbspn) mustard
90ml (6tbspns) tomato purée
1 handful of finely chopped parsley
2.5ml (1/2tspn) finely chopped sage
15ml (1tbspn) crushed bay leaves
Salt and ground black pepper to taste

Sauté the finely chopped onions in butter until they are a golden colour, then add the ham and the beef, stirring all the time. Add the carrots, mushrooms, salt and pepper to taste, the beef stock and gravy and mustard, tomato purée and herbs. Simmer gently for 40 minutes. Place in ovenproof dish. Cook the green peas for 2 minutes and then place them in a layer on top of the meat mixture. Cook and mash the potatoes, adding butter, salt and pepper. Place the potatoes on top of the mixture and cook at 200C, 400F or Gas Mark 6 for 30 minutes or until the potatoes are crispy on top. Allow to cool and place in the refrigerator overnight. Serve cold for lunch at the ground in front of the thatched pavilion.

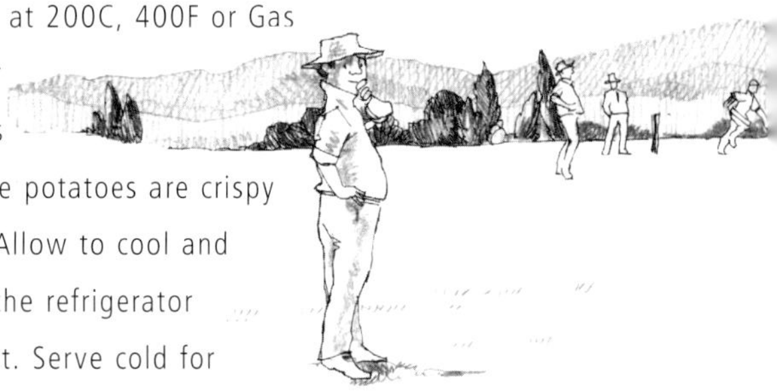

Richie Benaud
Coogee, NSW, Australia

CHICKEN AND MUSHROOM KEDGEREE

1kg (2.2lb) long-grained rice
12 hard-boiled eggs, chopped
225g (8oz) butter or margarine
450g (1lb) button mushrooms, sliced
1kg (2.2lb) cooked chicken, chopped
568ml (1 pint) double cream
Salt and black pepper
Parsley, chopped

Cook the rice in boiling salted water for about 10 minutes until just tender, drain and leave covered. Melt the butter or margarine in a large pan and add mushrooms. Cook gently until softened and then add rice, cooked chicken, cream and chopped eggs. Add salt and pepper to taste. Heat through and serve sprinkled with chopped parsley. Serves approximately 30.

Mrs. Judy Martin-Jenkins

QUICK CHEESE PIZZA

Dough
225g (8oz) self-raising flour
5ml (1tspn) salt
30ml (2tbspns) cooking oil
105ml (7tbspns) cold water

Topping
Tomato Paste
Onions
Mushrooms
Peppers
Tomatoes
Grated cheese
Oregano

Preheat oven to 190C, 375F or Gas Mark 5. Mix the flour, oil, salt, water and oregano into a dough. Knead lightly and roll to fit greased flat 15"x10" tin. Spread with tomato paste, sliced onions, mushrooms, peppers and tomatoes. Cover with grated cheese and oregano. Bake for approximately 40 minutes.

Mrs. Pamela Leaf
Walton Cricket Club, Wetherby, West Yorkshire

"I'm confident they play the game (and take tea) in Heaven. Wouldn't be Heaven otherwise, would it?"

Patrick Moore, TV Astronomer, Leg-spinner and No.11 bat

HASH PIE

700g (1 1/2lb) potatoes
1 medium onion
340g (12oz) tin corned beef,
225g (8oz) shortcrust pastry
Salt, pepper & herbs

Preheat oven to 190C, 375F or Gas Mark 5. Peel and finely chop potatoes and onion. Place in a large saucepan and add salt to taste. Boil for 20 minutes. Place corned beef in large bowl and mash. Drain potatoes and onion and mash. Add to corned beef and mix until combined. Grease and line 10" flan dish with pastry, reserving trimmings. Spoon corned beef mixture into pastry and level top. Use pastry trimmings to form lattice on top of pie. Bake for 30 minutes. Serve hot or cold.

Mrs. K. Sant
Whitmore Cricket Club, Staffordshire

One day the Second XI was fortunate to have the services of a 12th man who otherwise unemployed was delegated to light the boiler, cut the sandwiches, butter the scones etc, while his team mates were out in the field. With a few overs until the tea interval and conscious of the need to have the tea brewed when the players came off the field, he interrupted play to enquire how many tea bags were required for the pot. "10" was the reply, which for standard-size tea bags was the right number for the size of the teapot. Unfortunately the tea bags were "catering-size" ones - there wasn't much room left for any water and you can imagine the colour and strength of the tea! The person concerned has never been entrusted with 'catering duties' since!

Walton Cricket Club, Yorkshire

VEGETARIAN PASTA BAKE

400g (14oz) pasta twirls
1 small onion, diced
4 cups mushrooms, sliced
1/2 broccoli (divided into florets, cooked for 5 minutes and drained)
2 x 400g (14oz) cans chopped tomatoes
2 medium courgettes (cut into rustic chunks, cooked for 5 minutes and drained)
1 clove garlic
5ml (1tspn) chilli purée or large pinch of chilli powder
5ml (1tspn) tomato purée
225g (1/2lb) Cheddar cheese, grated
1/2 cup breadcrumbs, fresh if possible
15ml (1tbspn) oregano
Paprika, salt, pepper and butter

Start by boiling the broccoli and courgettes, drain, rinse in cold water and drain again. Melt a knob of butter in a large saucepan, add the diced onion and cook on a medium heat for about 10 minutes. Add the garlic and mushrooms and cook for an additional minute or two. Pour in the chopped tomatoes, tomato purée, chilli purée/powder, oregano, salt and pepper. Simmer on a medium heat for 15 minutes. Cook the pasta, and place in a large oven proof dish. Add the cooked vegetables and pour over the tomato mixture. Mix the breadcrumbs, Cheddar cheese and paprika together and sprinkle generously over the dish. Grill until the topping is golden brown and the centre is piping hot.

Mrs. Patricia Ross-Hurst
Army Cricket Association, Aldershot, Hampshire

CHICKEN AND SWEETCORN FLAN

1 small onion, finely chopped
25g (1oz) butter
25g (1oz) flour
2.5ml (1/2tspn) dry mustard
2.5ml (1/2tspn) salt and pepper mixed
150ml (1/4pint) milk
200g (7oz) can sweetcorn with peppers
100g (4oz) diced cooked chicken
30ml (2tbspns) cream
25-50g (1-2oz) grated cheese
Pastry to line 8" flan case

Preheat oven to 200C, 400F or Gas Mark 6. Bake the 8" flan case "blind" for 20 minutes only. Fry the onion in butter until soft but not coloured. Stir in flour, mustard, salt and pepper and cook for 1 minute. Drain sweetcorn, add liquid to milk. Stir this into onion mixture in the pan. Bring to boil and cook for 2 minutes. Remove from heat. Mix in the sweetcorn, chicken, cream and add extra seasoning to taste. Pour into the partly-cooked, hot flan case and cover top with cheese. Return to moderately hot oven for 12-14 minutes until cheese is melted and turning golden. Can be eaten hot or cold. To reheat flan, cover with foil and put in moderately hot oven for 12-15 minutes

Mrs. Siân Jones
Carew Cricket Club, Pembrokeshire

BEEF, POTATO AND ONION PIE

Pastry
450g (1lb) flour
225g (8oz) lard

Filling
700g (1 1/2lb) pasty beef or lean minced beef
4 large potatoes, chopped
1 large onion, chopped
Salt and pepper
1 egg beaten, for glaze

Preheat oven to 200C, 400F or Gas Mark 6. Make pastry and roll out 2 rounds to fit a round 8" greased tin. Mix well by hand all the other ingredients in a large bowl. Place mixture on to pastry base and put the other round of pastry on top, sealing the edges with a little milk. Glaze with beaten egg. Cook for approximately 1 hour on top shelf to start with then middle shelf on slightly cooler heat.

Mrs. M. R. Gead
Boconnoc Cricket Club, Cornwall

After cricket, no ceremony in the English canon is conducted with quite the reverence of tea; and after tea, cricket. Nothing then is more appropriate to the summer game than the tea interval which interrupts it. It is as important as the whiteness of flannels, the taking of the guard, the squareness of the legs, the signal of fours: while those who muster the tea are as revered as the umpires.

Neil Durden-Smith. From The Lord's Taverners Sticky Wicket Book (Queen Anne Press)

PAULA'S PASTIES

Pastry
900g (2lb) self-raising flour
225g (8oz) margarine
225g (8oz) lard
Cold water as necessary

Filling
1.5kg (3 1/2lb) potatoes
2 x 340g (12oz) tins corned beef
2-3 onions to taste
1 egg, beaten
Herbs
Salt & black pepper

Preheat oven to 170C, 325F or Gas Mark 3. Rub fat into flour to make fine breadcrumbs. Add water until a dough-like mixture is made. Put into fridge until required. Cook and mash potatoes. Add corned beef and onions, mixing together. Roll out pastry and cut into 4" diameter circles. Brush around outer edge with egg and then add a dessertspoonful of filling to centre. Pull the pastry edges together to form a ridge and crimp together. Brush the top of the pasty with egg for glaze. Place on a baking tray and bake until golden brown. Makes approximately 60 pasties.

Mrs. Paula Ralph
Carew Cricket Club, Pembrokeshire

"Bringing on the heavy roller . . "

THE CRICKET MATCH

Mothers, lovers, spreaders, slic

Dappled shade beneath the willows,
Clapped applause for boundary won,
Sound of ball on bat resounding,
Shining whites in English sun.

Village gathers for the combat,
Coloured rugs upon the grass;
Cows look up from peaceful grazing,
New lambs frolic as they pass.

Fathers strive with ball of leather,
Spinning, twisting, Yorkers straight,
Facing foe before the wicket,
Crouching low in field to wait.

Children make believe they're heroes,
Play for England, super-star;
'Gainst the fastest Aussie bowler
Hitting sixes super far.

Mothers, lovers, spreaders, slicers,
In the old pavilion toil;
Cakes and pastries, freshest sandwich,
Laden tables, kettles boil.

Long the day and far the shadows,
Hard the battle lost and won;
Sweet the dream of fellow players
Gathered in the local 'Crown'.

Silent now the pitch in moonlight,
Distant owl calls through the dark;
Fierce debate on every over
Lasts until the rising lark.

Richenda Goldfinch, 1998. Slieve Donard, Jerdacuttup, Western Australia

TANDOORI CHICKEN DRUMSTICKS

30 chicken drumsticks
Remove skin. Cut slits in flesh and set aside.

<u>Marinade</u>
750ml (1 1/2tspn) cumin seed
Seed from 2-3 cardomom pods
4 cloves
Grind above ingredients into powder and add

15ml (1tbspn) paprika
1 or 2 green chillies
3 garlic cloves, peeled
1 1/2" piece fresh ginger, peeled

Place above 4 marinade ingredients in a blender and mix to a paste with a little water.

60ml (4tbspns) plain yoghurt
10ml (2tspns) salt

Combine powder and paste and mix with 60ml (4tbspns) plain yoghurt and salt in a large bowl. Add chicken drumsticks. Cover and marinade for at least 12 hours. On morning of match place chicken on a tray and cook in a hot oven for about 30 minutes or until tender.

Mrs. Angharad Merwah
Pontblyddyn Cricket Club, Flintshire

We had the obligatory streaker on one Sunday afternoon a few seasons ago. She came from behind the pavilion, ran diagonally across the pitch and jumped into a car which was travelling slowly along the road bordering our ground. The captain missed the entire incident, however, because he was in the pavilion putting on the tea urn!

Ley Hill Cricket Club, Buckinghamshire

TABBOULEH

1kg (2lb5oz) bulgar wheat
1700ml (60fl.oz) boiling water
25ml (5tspns) salt
2.25kg (5lbs) tomatoes chopped
2 1/2 cucumbers, diced
2 bunches spring onions chopped
Salt and freshly ground black pepper

For the dressing
250ml (10fl.oz) olive oil
250ml (10fl.oz) lemon juice
150ml (10tbspns) fresh mint, finely chopped
5-10 cloves garlic, crushed
90ml (6tbspns) fresh parsley, finely chopped

Mix the bulgar wheat with the salt, pour over the boiling water and leave it for 15-20 minutes. The wheat will swell and absorb the water. (Alternatively, for a crunchier salad, you can use cold water, leaving it to soak for longer). If all the water is not absorbed, drain through sieve and then wring it in a clean tea towel.

Mix the dressing ingredients together and pour the mixture over the soaked bulgar, then leave it overnight in a refrigerator or cool place. Next day fold in the salad ingredients, top with fresh parsley and serve. Serves 30.

Mrs. Jill Wilson
Yorkshire and England

MISQUOTES
BY UNDER ARM

I wandered lonely at third man
Until the clock struck four
Then all at once I saw a crowd
That in for tea had gone before.

Wordsworth

ZESTY LEG OF LAMB

2kg (4 1/2lb) leg of lamb
1/4 cup mango chutney
30ml (2tbspns) French mustard
2 garlic cloves crushed
15ml (1tbspn) red wine vinegar
15ml (1tbspn) Worcester sauce

Preheat oven to 200C, 400F or Gas Mark 6. Trim large pieces of fat from lamb. Place meat on rack in baking dish. Combine chutney, mustard, garlic, vinegar and Worcester sauce in a pan. Cook for 3-4 minutes until bubbling. Using a brush coat the lamb with half the mixture. Shield the shank end of the lamb with smooth foil strips. Place in preheated oven at 200C, 400F, or Gas Mark 6 for 1 hour then drop the temperature to 150C, 300F or Gas Mark 2 for another 2 hours, or until a thermometer inserted in the centre reaches 57 degrees for medium rare. Halfway through cooking remove the foil and turn meat over and brush with remaining mixture. Transfer lamb to platter and cover with foil and allow to stand.

Serve with new potatoes, chopped chives and spring vegetables.

Serves 8.

Georgie Murfitt
The Willows Cricket Club, Loburn, North Canterbury, New Zealand

BACON AND EGG QUICHE

Pastry Base
175g (6oz) plain flour
75g (3oz) butter or margarine
Pinch of salt

Filling
175g (6oz) streaky bacon
2 eggs
1/4 pint (5fl.oz) single cream
175g (6oz) English Cheddar cheese

Preheat oven to 220C, 425F or Gas Mark 7. Sift flour and salt into bowl. Rub in butter until mixture is like breadcrumbs. Add enough cold water to make into a firm dough. Roll out onto lightly floured surface. Line an 8" flan dish and place it on baking tray. Chop the bacon up and place across the pastry base. Beat the eggs, fresh cream and grated cheese together. Pour this mixture over the bacon. Place in the oven. Cook at 220C, 425F or Gas Mark 7 for 10 minutes. Reduce the heat to 190C, 375F or Gas Mark 5 and cook for a further 20-30 minutes until set and golden brown in colour. Can be served hot or cold.

Mrs. Susan Turner
Hambledon Cricket Club, Hampshire

Jonathan Agnew, BBC Test Match Special Commentator
"I don't know Bill - can you send cake by e-mail?"

CHICKEN WITH ASPARAGUS SPEARS

10 x 425g (15oz) cans asparagus spears, drained
3750g (7 1/2lb) cooked chicken, roughly shredded
10 x 275g (10oz) cans condensed cream of chicken soup
875ml (1 1/2 pints) or large 800g jar Hellmann's mayonnaise
25ml (5tspns) curry powder
Freshly ground black pepper, to taste
500g (20oz) Cheddar cheese, grated
275g (10oz) butter
20 thick slices of white or brown bread, crusts removed and cubed
15ml (1tbspn) lemon juice
Chopped parsley

Preheat oven to 190C, 375F or Gas Mark 5. Arrange the asparagus spears evenly over the base of well-buttered gratin dishes or foil freezer containers. Place the chicken in a layer over the asparagus. Combine the soup, mayonnaise, curry powder, lemon juice and pepper in a bowl, then pour the mixture over the chicken. Sprinkle the grated cheese over the top of the dish. Melt the butter in a large saucepan, then remove from the heat. Do not allow it to brown. Add the cubes of bread to the melted butter and toss them gently until they are well soaked. Arrange the bread and chopped parsley over the cheese. Place in oven and cook for 45 minutes until heated through and crisp on top. Serves 30.

Mrs. Ana West
Bluemantles Cricket Club, Tunbridge Wells, Kent

CURRIED CHICKEN SALAD

142ml (1/4pint) yoghurt (preferably Greek)
75-90ml (5/6 tbspns) Hellmann's mayonnaise
10ml (1dsspn) mild curry powder, to taste
10ml (2tspns) dried tarragon
10ml (2tspns) seasoning salt
2 small onions
4 sticks celery
2 red peppers
450g (1lb) cooked chicken, chopped into bite-sized pieces
2/3 bananas, sliced
Red pepper for garnish

Mix the yoghurt and mayonnaise together with the curry powder, seasoning, salt and tarragon. Stir in onion rings, celery, chopped pepper and chicken. Chill in fridge. Before serving stir in banana slices. Garnish with red pepper slices. Serve with other salad dishes or poppadoms. If you want to keep the cost down, reduce the chicken and add more salad or banana ingredients. Serves 8-10 people.

Mrs. Wendy Bachelor
Failand and Portbury Cricket Club, Bristol

At Taunton in 1946, on the third day of a county game, a wicket fell and the fielding side waited for the next batsman to appear. To their amazement, instead of a batsman, a lady with an umbrella and a huge picnic basket appeared down the pavilion steps. She walked straight through the fielders and calmly disappeared into the crowd!

Christopher Martin-Jenkins. From The Cricketer Book of Cricket Eccentrics and Eccentric Behaviour. (Lennard Books)

CHILLI CON CARNE

4.5kg (10lb) chuck steak, cut into very small pieces and oil for frying
9 Spanish onions, chopped
10 cloves of garlic, crushed
7 beef stock cubes, dissolved in 3 pints of water
8 x 400g (14oz) tins chopped tomatoes
340g (12oz) jar tomato purée
10 fresh chillies, chopped and deseeded
40ml (2 1/2tbspns) chilli powder
45ml (3tbspns) ground cinnamon
225g (8oz) plain chocolate, melted in a little water
120ml (8tbspns) plain flour
4 red peppers, chopped and deseeded
2 green peppers, chopped and deseeded
9 x 400g (14oz) tins red kidney beans

Brown the beef in the oil and remove from heat. Drain on kitchen paper. Lower the heat and fry the onions and garlic until transparent. Replace the beef in the casserole with the onions and garlic. Sprinkle in the flour and chilli powder and stir until incorporated. Mix the tomato purée and stock and add slowly to the beef and onion mixture. Add the tinned tomatoes, cinnamon, chillies, chocolate and peppers. Stir till well-mixed. Season and simmer for approximately 3 hours (if using one large catering pan) or until thoroughly cooked and tender. Finally, drain the kidney beans and add to the casserole, heat through. Serve with 2.5kg (5lbs) cooked rice and, if liked, guacamole and corn chips. Serves 30.

Mrs. Roz Bairamian
Bluemantles Cricket Club, Tunbridge Wells, Kent

QUICK QUICHE

Pastry

3/4 cup shortcrust pastry mix

Filling

1 cup milk

3/4 cup chopped bacon

3/4 cup cheese, grated

3/4 cup onion, chopped

Salt and pepper

3 eggs, beaten

Preheat oven to 180C, 350F or Gas Mark 4. Place all ingredients in a bowl. Mix together. Line greased flan dish with rolled out pastry. Pour in mixture. Slice a tomato on the top and bake for 30-35 minutes.

Mrs. Alison Ford
Bishops Cannings Cricket Club, Wiltshire

Mrs. Beryl Maw, who retired from tea duties after 40 years missed only two Saturdays and in that time she would have boiled 3,840 eggs!

Cayton Cricket Club, North Yorkshire

SAVOURY PLAIT

Pastry

225g (8oz) self-raising flour

150g (5oz) lard

1.25ml (1/4tspn) salt

Approx. 142ml (1/4 pint) water

1 egg for glaze

Filling

450g (1lb) sausagemeat

2 medium onions fried in butter

5ml (1tspn) sage

15ml (1tbspn) water

Salt and pepper

Preheat oven to 220C, 425F or Gas Mark 7. Make pastry and place in fridge. Blend filling ingredients together with salt and pepper to taste. Roll out pastry and place on greased tin before adding the filling, fold over and brush with beaten egg. Bake for 35 minutes until golden brown. Makes 2 Savoury Plaits, 24 slices.

Mrs. Kathleen Mangham
Wadworth Cricket Club, South Yorkshire

We have a non-playing member who is the owner of a dog - a Yorkshire Terrier called "Vinny" who is an incredible finder of lost balls. Our field is next to the well-known Yorkshire rhubarb fields where it is impossible to find balls hit for 6. But on his daily walks Vinny will always sniff them out. In fact a few years ago, he was presented with a mounted ball at our annual presentations!

Carlton Cricket Club, Yorkshire

PORK GOULASH

5.5kg (12lb) pork shoulder, trimmed and cut into bite-sized pieces and oil for cooking
6 Spanish onions, chopped
10 cloves of garlic, crushed
4 red peppers, chopped and deseeded
2 green peppers, chopped and deseeded
6 x 400g (14oz) tins chopped tomatoes
150ml (10tbspns) plain flour
150ml (10tbspns) paprika
60ml (4tbspns) carraway seeds
60ml (4tbspns) dill seeds
60fl.oz (3pints) cider
60fl.oz (3pints) chicken stock
60fl.oz (3pints) soured cream

Brown pork in the oil and remove from pan. Drain on kitchen paper. Lower heat and fry the onions and garlic until transparent. Replace the pork in the casserole with the onions and garlic. Sprinkle in the flour and paprika and stir to incorporate. Add stock, carraway seeds, dill seeds and chopped peppers. Mix thoroughly. Season and simmer until tender (about 3 hours) in a large catering pan. Just before serving, add soured cream, stir to incorporate and heat through. Do not allow to boil. Serve with 2.5kg (5lb) cooked rice and cucumber and dill salad. Serves 30-40.

Mrs. Roz Bairamian
Bluemantles Cricket Club, Tunbridge Wells, Kent

I certainly don't consider myself a 'long suffering' tea lady but sometimes I feel as if I married the whole 1st XI!

Mrs. Kay Lawrenson. Overton-on-Dee Cricket Club

CORONATION CHICKEN

2 x 1.5kg (3lb) chickens
30ml (2tbpsns) olive oil
15-30ml (1-2 level tbspns) curry powder
284ml (1/2pint) of chicken stock (or use chicken stock cubes)
Juice of 1 lemon
60ml (4 rounded tbspns) apricot jam
568ml (1pint) Hellman's mayonnaise
1 large onion
20ml (1dsspn) tomato purée
60ml (4tbspns) mango chutney
Roasted flaked almonds (optional)

Cook chickens and strip them. Finely chop the onion and fry in heated oil for 5 minutes. Stir in curry powder and cook for a further 2 minutes. Add stock, tomato purée, lemon juice, chutney and jam. Stir until boiling then simmer for 5 minutes. Place in a blender or liquidiser. Allow to cool then stir in mayonnaise. Mix into the chicken. Garnish with roasted almonds (optional) and parsley. Serves 10.

Mrs. Charmaine Hutton
The Cricketer, Beech Hanger, Ashurst, Kent

HADDOCK MAYONNAISE

3kg (6 1/2lb) smoked haddock fillet
400g (14oz) jar Hellmann's mayonnaise
400g (14oz) fromage frais
2 red peppers, finely diced (optional)
6 hard-boiled eggs, chopped
2 cucumbers
Parsley
Salt and black pepper

Pour boiling water over the smoked haddock fillet and leave to cool completely. Skin and flake the fish. Mix the other ingredients in a bowl and fold in the fish. Serve piled on a flat dish surrounded by a ring of thinly sliced cucumbers. Decorate with parsley. Serves approximately 30.

Mrs. Judy Martin-Jenkins

Test Umpires David Constant and Alan Whitehead refused to leave the field during the tea interval of Hampshire's John Player League match with Essex in 1984. They sat on the square as a way of making the point that a reduction in the tea interval to just fifteen minutes made it impossible for them to get and drink a cup of tea, quite apart from anything else they may wish to do. On the day of their protest, tea was taken out to the umpires.

Christopher Martin-Jenkins, BBC Test Match Special Commentator. From The Cricketer Book of Cricket Eccentrics and Eccentric Behaviour. (Lennard Books)

RICE AND TOMATO SALAD

90ml (6tbspns) long-grained rice
8 tomatoes, skinned
30ml (2tbspns) chopped parsley
30ml (2tbspns) lemon juice
10ml (2tspns) French mustard
10ml 2tspns) caster sugar
Salt and ground black pepper
100g (4oz) button mushrooms, thinly sliced
60ml (4tbspns) olive oil
1 clove garlic, crushed
15ml (3tspns) chopped basil

Cook rice in boiling salted water until tender. Cool under running water. Chop tomatoes, discarding seeds. Put rice, tomatoes and mushrooms into a bowl and sprinkle over parsley. Mix oil, lemon juice and garlic together. Blend in the mustard, basil, sugar, salt and pepper. Spoon the dressing over the rice and mix well. Cover and chill until needed. Serve with green salad from a choice of lettuce, green peppers, cucumbers, celery, courgettes, cress etc. Serves 10.

Mrs. Charmaine Hutton
The Cricketer, Beech Hanger, Ashurst, Kent

THE CRICKETER MAYONNAISE

This is a wonderful base for many different sandwiches, salads and dips. It is also very popular with my family and their friends. It takes about a minute to make in a liquidiser.

If you are worried about salmonella do not make it. I use good eggs from a reliable source without any problem and always store the mayonnaise in a container in the fridge.

1 egg, size 2, at room temperature
5ml (1tspn) grain mustard - (or Dijon)
5ml (1tspn) caster or granulated sugar
20ml (2dsspns) cider vinegar
2 cloves garlic (optional)
284ml (1/2 pint) sunflower oil
Salt & ground black pepper

Put all the above except the OIL in the liquidiser and turn on to full speed for 1/4 minute to mix well. Slowly pour into the mixture about 284ml (1/2 pint) oil, while the liquidiser is still turned on at fast (not full) speed. (Do not use olive oil as flavour is too strong). Continue pouring oil until the mayonnaise thickens well.

Note: If the mayonnaise separates, which can happen if the egg yolk is too cold or too much vinegar or oil is added too fast, do not worry. Tip mixture into a jug, add another egg and a teaspoon of vinegar to the liquidiser, turn on fast and slowly add the curdled mixture. Normally it turns into smooth mayonnaise.

To vary the Mayonnaise flavours

Add a good handful of fresh parsley, dill, thyme, sage - no need to chop as this will be done in the liquidiser before adding the oil.

Add 20ml (1dsspn) mild curry paste to ingredients before adding the oil.

Add 40ml (2dsspns) tomato ketchup to ingredients before adding the oil.

Add generous bunch of tarragon

Add 40ml (2dsspns) Dijon mustard

The mayonnaise is delicious mixed with hard-boiled or scrambled eggs, or tuna, tinned salmon, prawns, cream cheese and salad to fill sandwiches.

Mrs. Belinda Brocklehurst
The Cricketer, Beech Hanger, Ashurst, Kent

SPECIAL CAYTON SANDWICHES

1. Take four slices of bread and butter each slice.
On first slice, place lettuce, tomato and cucumber.
On second slice, place egg mayonnaise and put on top of first slice.
On third slice, put luncheon meat or beef or ham and chutney.
Top with fourth slice and cut into quarters and arrange with garnish.

2. Brown bread and butter: spread with cream cheese and prawns.

3. Mix a pinch of curry powder with butter and spread on bread, top up with sardines, sliced tomatoes and parsley.

4. Grate some cheese, mix with tomato sauce, a pinch of salt and spread on an open bread bun.

Mrs. June Farnaby
Cayton Cricket Club, North Yorkshire

It's the buttering of sandwiches, the ordering of pork pies, the gurgling of tea urns, the whitening of cricket boots, the sniffing of wind for rain, the echoing squirt of beer into empty glasses at the end of the match that give the day its proper flavour. There is a tendency to think of village cricket as a quaint bucolic outpost, supported by simpletons in smocks, played by beery cranks with big bellies.

Peter Tinniswood from "Portrait of Gowerton".

SAVOURY MIXTURE FOR SANDWICH FILLER

6 eggs, hard-boiled
6 tomatoes, skinned
1 x 340g (12oz) tin ham or corned beef
Bunch of spring onions
Salt and pepper to taste
Mayonnaise

Mince eggs, tomatoes, ham and spring onions. Add seasoning and bind with mayonnaise. For a more economical filling, omit tomatoes and ham and use 8 eggs per loaf of bread. Sufficient for 1 loaf.

Mrs. Mary Evans
Pontblyddyn Cricket Club, Flintshire

Sandwiches are but the beginning of a tea ladies toil, the bread and butter of devotion, though they have been the end of too many a budding romance.

Judith Chalmers, Lady Taverner. From The Lord's Taverners Sticky Wicket Book (Queen Anne Press)

DIPS FOR CRISPS, TORTILLA CHIPS OR CHEESE BISCUITS

Using Home-made Cricketer mayonnaise as base:
Mix with mashed avocado and a little lemon juice.
Mashed baked aubergine peeled and well-drained before mixing with a little lemon juice.
Mix with prawns, lemon juice and tomato ketchup.
Mix with cream cheese and chopped chives.

Mrs. Belinda Brocklehurst
The Cricketer, Beech Hanger, Ashurst, Kent

GOOD SANDWICH FILLER

2 eggs
2 spring onions, sliced
75ml (5tbspns) salad cream/mayonnaise
200g (7oz) can tuna
2.5ml (1/2 level tspn) salt
1.25ml (1/4 level tspn) pepper

Hard boil the eggs and chop. Mix together above ingredients with salad cream/mayonnaise. Keeps well in a refrigerator for 3 days and is more popular than plain tuna or egg and lettuce.

Mrs. Margaret Flintoff (Snr.)
Sessay Cricket Club, Yorkshire

It is estimated that there are 50,000 cricket clubs in Britain. If each plays on average once a weekend, there are half a million matches a summer. If each player's ration is one sandwich per game, cricket consumes twenty-two million slices of cut loaf before the spectators have had a bite. The loaves could pave a hundred acres!

Judith Chalmers. Lady Taverner. From The Lord's Taverners Sticky Wicket Book (Queen Anne Press)

HAYSLIP

450g (1lb) sausagemeat
1 small packet sage and onion stuffing mix
3 slices of dry bread
1 cup of boiling water
1 egg
Dried herbs (optional)

Preheat oven to 180C, 350F or Gas Mark 4. Mix all ingredients together. Place in a greased 450g (1lb) loaf tin. Cook for approximately 1 1/2 - 2 hours. When cold slice and fill 2 loaves of bread. Serve with salad or mustard pickle.

Mrs. J. Garley
Geddington Cricket Club, Northamptonshire

A useful borrowing from American sport

"How long before tea?"

The tea itself is something of an occasion in its own right. For this special event the Stebbing tea-ladies have made a special effort. The sandwiches, tongue and cucumber, egg and lettuce. cream cheese and cress, ham and tomato-are as soft as feather pillows, but this is far from all. There are flaky pastry sausage rolls, vol-au-vents, biscuits with olives in the middle, and all this is just for starters. Beyond them are the ranks of cakes lined up for afters-thick chocolate cake with thick chocolate icing, cherry cake, madeira cake, seed cake, treacle tart, apple dumpling, sponge roll, peanut nuggets, ginger biscuits, Scotch shortbread. There is much more of this than twenty-two cricketers can consume, and before long plates of goodies and trays of teacups begin to circulate among the guests, visitors and camp followers.

Robert Holles. From The Guide to Real Village Cricket

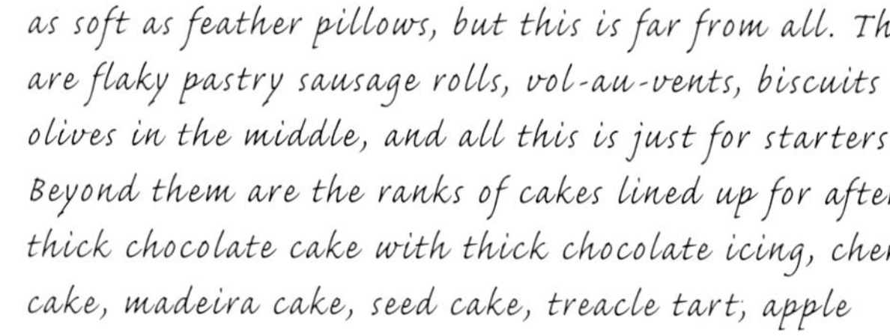

Cricket tea recipes - thirst quenchers

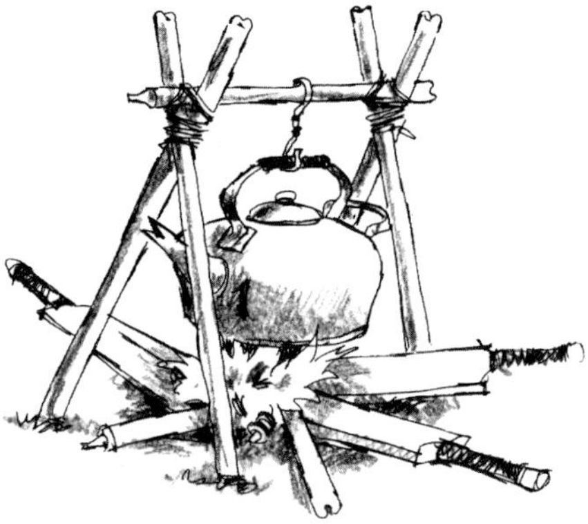

TEA

Allow 1 standard-sized tea bag per person in a large tea pot. Top up afterwards with 2-3 more tea bags and more water for a second cup. Allow 3-4 pints milk for an average team plus a few spectators. Sugar. Use mugs to save on washing up.

Some people may prefer coffee or lemon tea, so have a jar of coffee and a lemon handy.

MISQUOTES

BY UNDER ARM

" Of course I'll make tea; I'd have made it even if you'd asked me"

Not actually a misquote, but overheard of self!

ELDERFLOWER CORDIAL

20 elderflower heads, shaken and washed
2kg (4 1/2lb) sugar
1 litre (1 3/4 pints) boiling water
50g (2oz) citric acid (available from chemists)
2 lemons, grated, then sliced

Stir sugar into boiling water and melt sugar. Add citric acid, grated rind of lemons and then sliced lemons. Pour into a bowl. Add elderflower heads and leave overnight covered with plastic film or piece of foil. Sieve out the flowers and pour syrup through a jelly bag or muslin cloth to clarify. Put into screw-top plastic bottles and store in fridge at all times. Can be frozen in small bottles. The elderflowers must be open, creamy white and not blown or dropping.

To serve: Dilute one-part of the syrup with eight parts of sparkling or plain mineral water. Can be mixed with gin and soda water or make a Spritzer with elderflower cordial, soda and wine, add a sprig of mint and serve with ice. Can be used to flavour gooseberry dishes, fruit salads and ices.

Mrs. Charmaine Hutton
The Cricketer, Beech Hanger, Ashurst, Kent

HOME-MADE LEMONADE

340g (12oz) sugar
15ml (1tbspn) finely grated lemon rind
340ml (12fl.oz) hot water
340ml (12fl.oz) lemon

Put sugar and lemon rind into a 1 litre (2 pint) capacity screw-top jar and add the water. Screw the top on tightly. Shake until the sugar is dissolved and add the lemon juice. Chill well. Serve with ice cubes, soda water or water and sliced lemons. Makes 3.7 litres / 6 1/2 pints.

ELDERFLOWER FIZ

12 elderflower heads, washed and free from insects
700g (1lb 9oz) white sugar
3 lemons
30ml (2tbpns) white wine vinegar
4.5litres (8 pints) water

Dissolve sugar in a little water heated to boiling. Thinly pare the lemons and add this peel to the sugar. Put the elderflower heads in a large earthenware or glass bowl. Then add the sugar and peel mixture, the white wine vinegar and remaining water. Stir well and leave for 4 days. Strain off the liquid and bottle. In 5 days or so it should be sparkling. Serve well chilled. Makes 5 litres / 9 pints.

This ultimate country drink is cheap to make and is made from the simplest ingredients. The elderflowers grow in abundance in early summer on the edge of the cricket field. It is a wonderful thirst quencher.

Mrs. Kay Lawrenson
Overton-on-Dee Cricket Club, Wrexham

CIDER CUP

2 litres (3 1/2 pints) medium dry cider
2 bottles dry white wine
2 litres (3 1/2 pints) lemonade
2 wine glasses Medium Dry Sherry
2 lemons, thinly sliced

Mix the ingredients together ensuring that everything is well chilled beforehand. Serves 30

CHILLED WINE TEA

30ml (6 tspns) Darjeeling tea
1.8 litre (3 pints) water
3 bottles dry white wine
1 handful of parings of orange rind
1 handful of sprigs of mint

Start to make this at least two hours before the tea interval. Make tea and leave to brew for 2-3 minutes. Strain the tea into a large jug and, when cool enough, chill in the fridge. Once chilled, add the wine, orange parings and mint and let them infuse before serving. Ice cubes may be added if wished.

Makes enough for 2 teams, umpires and one or two lucky hangers-on! Perfect when there is a heatwave.

Mrs Ana West
Bluemantles Cricket Club, Tunbridge Wells, Kent

MULLED WINE

568ml (1 pint) water
225g (8oz) sugar
8 cloves
2 x 5cm (2") cinnamon sticks
4 lemons, thinly sliced
2 bottles Burgundy or claret
2 oranges, thinly sliced

Put the water, sugar and spices into a large saucepan. Bring to boil. Remove from the heat and stir in the lemons. Leave to stand for 10 minutes. Add wine and heat through without boiling. Strain into a heated punch bowl, add the orange slices and serve hot. Makes 900ml / 1 1/2 pints.

Excellent for cold April match days to warm up the players and spectators!

Having the other day, once again spent an afternoon in watching a village cricket match, I am again perplexed by the passion for that game which is displayed by those who cannot shine at it. They cannot bat, they cannot bowl, they leave their place in the field, they miss catches, they fumble returns; and yet every Saturday, there they are, often in perfect flannels, ready to fail once more."

E.V.Lucas, 1908

HOME-MADE PIMM'S

1 bottle red Cinzano
1 bottle Gin
1 bottle Medium Dry Sherry
2 litres (3 1/2 pints) lemonade
2 litres (3 1/2 pints), or more to taste, soda water
1 lemon, sliced
1 orange, sliced
1/2 cucumber, sliced
Angostura Bitters (to taste)
Mint leaves
Ice cubes

Pour the bottles of Cinzano, Gin and Sherry into a large jug or bowl and add sliced fruit, cucumber and mint. Leave to soak for a few hours to bring out the flavour. Add soda water, lemonade and ice just before serving, and top with sprigs of mint.

This recipe is a lot cheaper than buying bottles of Pimm's and tastes much the same.

This is what, for Englishmen, cricket does. It draws together, in a little space of time and space, all the diverse arts of love and emulation, conflict and comradeship, patience and boldness, sunshine and shower, city and country, prose and poetry and maketh them one.

Sir Arthur Bryant

WEST INDIES RUM PUNCH

One of sour - lemon or lime
Two of sweet - brown sugar or clear syrup
Three of strong - West Indian Dark Rum
Four of weak - water/ice

Pour over ice
Splash of Angostura
Dust of nutmeg

ENJOY WITH CAUTION!

Ian Hart
Nevis, West Indies

OUR UMPIRE

If you hear someone moan, and rant and rave,
There's a high probability that it's our umpire, Dave.
He's our resident weatherman; our prophet of doom,
And you'll hear him on Saturdays in the club, around noon.

He cuts and rolls and marks out the wicket;
Such is this man's passion for Harrowden's cricket.
But when he puts on that white coat and hat,
He becomes impartial - AND THAT IS THAT!

No fairer umpire could be found,
Even if you travelled to Lord's Cricket Ground.
He's one in a million, our Umpire Dave -
So please excuse him when he moans, and rants and raves!

Anne Freeman. Little Harrowden Cricket Club

SLOE GIN

Sloes, pricked, to fill an empty jar two-thirds full
225-275 (8-10oz) castor sugar
Gin

Wash the sloes removing any stalks and prick all over to allow the juice to escape. Fill a clean, empty bottle two-thirds full with the pricked sloes. Add to this the caster sugar and then fill with gin. Screw the cap on tightly and shake well. Shake the bottle once or twice a week and leave for 6 months. Strain the sloes from the gin and retain them. Re-bottle the Sloe Gin in a clean bottle.

As an added bonus, put the retained sloes into another bottle and fill with white wine. Leave for a day or two, drain and discard the sloes for an interesting wine 'digestif'.

Sloe Gin is marvellous after a cricket match, served in small glasses. The fruit of the Blackthorn, more commonly known as the May tree, is the size of a small damson, bluish-black in colour and very bitter. They should be harvested when ripe in the autumn.

THE PYJAMA GAME

As they went out to bat, the old cricketer sat
Half asleep in the club's new pavilion.
Then he leapt in alarm as he shouted "Pyjamas!"
And his face turned from pink to vermilion.

"Why, they're all dressed for bed!" he cried shaking his head
"And the only thing white is the ball.
Up against that black screen , they can hardly be seen-
And some overseas chaps, not at all!"

"What would Hutton have thought of this new-fangled sport
Or, for that matter, W.G?
I don't think I can stick it. Why it just isn't cricket
Barman, bring me a large G. and T."

He was past play-by date, so his drink came too late.
When the barman said: "Sorry to trouble you."
He fell out of his chair, both legs in the air,
Given out -from on high-lbw.

Up in heaven, he said: "It is as I was led
To believe-here all pitches are green,
And an angelic sight, they are all dressed in white,
Without one sponsor's name to be seen."

Christopher Curtis. North Yorkshire 1994

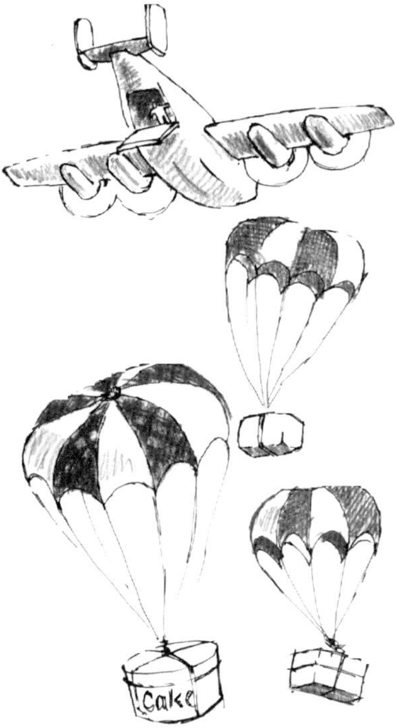

Cricket tea recipes - shopping lists

SHOPPING LIST FOR HARTLEY COUNTRY CLUB

Tea for 22 players, 2 umpires, 2 scorers, a few visitors and children

("Not too much, not too over the top as can be known and not too frugal as has also been known") from a cricket widow/mother/tea/lunch provider/scorer, washer of kit/ex driver of children to matches and coaching etc. etc!

USEFUL TIP

Four long sliced loaves of bread make 48 quartered sandwiches per loaf.

Fillings:

Egg mayonnaise with mustard and cress. Use 6 large eggs and one box of mustard and cress for 1 loaf.

Strongish Cheddar cheese and either onion, tomato or brown pickle.

Sliced ham with mustard or pickle (a dozen thickish slices).

Spreading paté with tomato.

Mashed softened corned beef (large tin), mixed with tomato ketchup or brown pickle.

Red or pink salmon, tuna or sardines, cucumber and salad cream/mayonnaise mashed.

Mixed salad sandwiches with tomato, cucumber, spring onions, iceberg lettuce, cress plus salad cream/mayonnaise.

18-24 scones with butter and jam in halves and, in season strawberries and fresh cream. Small cocktail sausage rolls and bowls of crisps if there are extra visitors.

Cakes: 2 x 3 egg-mix iced Victoria sandwich sponges, with jam and butter cream fillings. 1 large loaf tin-sized fruit cake cut into wedges. 2 dozen flapjacks. Battenburg cake, Swiss roll and jam tarts.

Cricket Lunch: 1.

Cold meat (slices of ham or turkey), or steak and kidney or chicken and mushroom pies and mixed salad with hot buttered new potatoes and French bread. Followed by trifle or strawberries and ice cream (in season) or apple tarts or flans. Also cheese and biscuits for the "non-pudding-minded" and coffee.

Cricket Lunch: 2.

Shepherd's pie made with baked beans, mushrooms, onions, Worcester sauce and tomato purée. Pile mashed potato on top with grated cheese and put under the grill until golden brown. Use large tins for roasting turkeys for 22 - 26 people and 1 1/2 bags of free flow mince (with soya) which, when mixed with the other ingredients bulks out well.

Mrs. Anne Senneck
Hartley Country Club, Kent

SHOPPING LIST FOR CAREW CRICKET CLUB

For 24 players, 2 scorers, 2 umpires and supporters

2 brown loaves, 3 white loaves, 2 dozen rolls cut in half to make open rolls, 6 eggs, 2 tins tuna, 675g (11/2lb) cheese, 675g (11/2lb) ham, lettuce, half a cucumber, 900g (2lb) tomatoes, 1 onion, 675g (11/2lb) margarine, 1.5lt (3 pints) milk.

These ingredients are used to make up a variety of filled sandwiches and open rolls. Cakes are given by our 3 duty Tea Ladies (rostered), who give on average 2 cakes each: (fruit cake, Madeira, lemon, chocolate, éclairs) or savoury flans or quiches.

SHOPPING LIST FOR CARLTON CRICKET CLUB

For 2 teams, 2 scorers, 2 umpires and two dozen supporters

2 dozen beef sandwiches (560g (11/4lb) beef)

2 dozen ham sandwiches (560g (11/4lb) ham)

2 dozen egg mayonnaise rolls topped with cress (6 eggs)

1 dozen long crusty rolls split and filled with grated cheese and tomato

2 dozen warm sausage rolls and sometimes, 2 dozen pieces of quiche.

Teas are served as a buffet. We have open sandwiches using Yorkshire tea-cakes (flat rolls about 3" diameter) cut in half and each half covered with lettuce, a slice of meat topped with tomato and cucumber. We usually have 4 large cakes, a plate of buttered scones, a tray of flapjacks or chocolate caramel biscuits, a plate of tarts or biscuits Each cake, (Victoria sponge, or chocolate) is cut into 10 pieces selling at 20 pence per slice. Tea, coffee, pop and crisps are also on sale. Sandwiches are 25 pence each.

SHOPPING LIST FOR WOODHOUSE GRANGE CRICKET CLUB

For 45 people

3 brown loaves, 3 white loaves, 10 eggs (if grated they will go further), 340g (12oz) cheese; 1 large tin pilchards; 10 slices ham; 10 slices turkey; 10 slices corned beef; I large bag frozen sausage rolls; 2 large square cakes (e.g. lemon and chocolate); 24 scones, 2 tray bakes. We allow 3 pieces of cake per person.

SHOPPING LIST FOR ST. ISHMAEL'S SPORTS AND SOCIAL CLUB

For players and spectators

Six loaves bread, (4 white, 2 wholemeal), 1 large Flora margarine, 450g (1lb) cooked ham, 450g (1lb) cheese, 1 jar sweet pickle, 1 tin corned beef, 1 tin tuna, 1/2 cucumber, 225g (1/2lb) tomatoes, 6 eggs, mayonnaise, cress, 2 dozen sausage parcels.

Cakes: 2 dozen jam and cream scones, coconut slices, lemon-topped mince pies, 8" boiled fruit cake, 1 dozen slices of coffee and walnut sponge cake, 1 dozen slices plain sponge cake with butter cream.

SHOPPING LIST FOR CAYTON CRICKET CLUB

Interesting sandwiches with different fillings (See page 90). Selections of butterfly buns, almond tarts, fruit cake, coconut buns, meringues, apricot walnut bread, Swiss rolls or American cheese cake. Scones: plain, cheese or cherry.

SHOPPING LIST FOR LANGWITH CRICKET CLUB

Buffet Tea for 26 people

2 dozen cob rolls, 1 white loaf, 1 brown loaf, 6 bags assorted crisps, 1 bag sausage rolls (party-size), 2 bags frozen chicken drumsticks, 225g (1/2lb) thin sliced ham, 225g (1/2lb) thick sliced beef, 6 eggs, 1 dozen Scotch eggs, 2 dishes tossed salad, salad cream, cucumber/onions soaked in vinegar, two large home-made fruit pies with custard or cream.

Sit Down Tea for 26 people

4 lettuces, 1/2 cucumber, 10 large tomatoes, 2 bunches celery, 2 bunches spring onions, 450g (1lb) red cheese, 225g (1/2lb) thin sliced ham, 1 large pork pie sliced, 3 loaves white bread, 1 loaf brown wholemeal bread. 36 assorted home-made buns, 1 home-made sponge and 1 chocolate sponge cake. Large salad cream, medium beetroot and a medium jar mixed pickles.

USEFUL ADVICE FROM THE BLUEMANTLES CRICKET CLUB TEA LADIES

1. To keep sandwiches as fresh as possible before the match wrap the uncut stack in cling film and surround it with a damp tea towel. Slices of cucumber on top of the fresh bread will also keep them moist.
2. The best way to cut a stack of sandwiches and to easily remove the crusts is to use an electric carving knife.
3. Three loaves of sliced bread with fillings is adequate for the average cricket tea.

NOTES AND OWN RECIPES

"Some hold that you can never make enough tea. . ."

Comparative Oven Temperatures

Very Slow	115-135C	200-280F	Gas 1/4-1/2
Slow	135-160C	280-320F	Gas 1
Warm	160-170C	320-340F	Gas 3
Moderate	170-185C	340-370F	Gas 4
Fairly Hot	185-205C	370-400F	Gas 5-6
Hot	205-225C	400-440F	Gas 7
Very Hot	225-250C	440-500F	Gas 8-9

Equivalent Measures

	(Working approximation)
1oz (28.35g)	25g
2oz (56.7g)	50g
4oz (113.4g)	100g
8oz (226.8g)	225g
12oz (340.2g)	350g
1lb (453.6g)	450g
1 kilo (2.2lb)	2 1/4lb
1oz flour	3 level tablespoons
1oz sugar	2 level tablespoons
1oz icing sugar	3 level tablespoons
1 1/2oz syrup	1 level tablespoon
1oz gelatine	2 1/2 level tablespoons
1oz butter	2 level tablespoons

1/4 pint (142ml)	5fl.oz	150ml
1/2 pint (284ml)	10fl.oz	300ml
1 pint (568ml)	20fl.oz	600ml
1/2 litre (0.88 pints)	18fl.oz	
1 litre (1.76 pints)	35fl.oz	1 3/4 pints
1 gallon		4.5 litres
1fl.oz		25ml
4fl.oz		100ml-125ml
8fl.oz		225ml

8. "Drinking the best tea in the world on an empty cricket ground - that, I think, is the final pleasure left to man". C.P.Snow

The editor acknowledges with gratitude those who have given permission for the use of copyright material. Every effort has been made to trace all copyright holders and the editor apologises to anyone who has not been found or properly acknowledged.

Hugh Cushing - Artist & Illustrator

After 15 years in North America practicing architecture, Hugh Cushing returned to Europe to live in France in 1980. There he began sketching his village boules team. Now back in England, Hugh's work includes most sports that people play; but in particular, Cricket! Each summer, from Lord's to village greens, he draws and paints, not only the players on the field, but all who come to watch from the boundary. His artistic travels have taken him to New Zealand and Australia, and he has done work for Kent players Chris Penn and Alan Igglesden's Testimonials. His original sketches for Cream Cakes and Boundaries catch the mood and joy of the game and have contributed hugely to the success of the book.